Deep Magic

By the same author

Seeds of Magick (with Catherine Summers)

The InnerSpace Workbook (with Catherine Summers)

Self-development with the Tarot (with Catherine Summers)

Pharmakon – Drugs and the Imagination

Now That's What I Call Chaos Magick (with Greg Humphries)

Magick Works

The Book of Baphomet (with Nikki Wyrd)

Deep Magic

Begins Here . . .

Julian Vayne

Copyright © 2013 Mandrake & Julian Vayne
First edition

All rights reserved. No part of this work may be reproduced or utilized in any form by any means electronic or mechanical, including *xerography, photocopying, microfilm,* and *recording,* or by any information storage system without permission in writing from the publishers.

The events depicted in this book are for entertainment purposes only and in no way reflect the actual life-style of any persons living or dead (including the author).

Cover photograph of Baphomet by Simon Costin

theblogofbaphomet.com

Contents

Deep Magic Begins Here… 7
The Pain of Division 9
The Sabbat of Chaos 16
Mastering Witchcraft 21
Dredd Lord of the Shadows 36
Jerusalem 43
The Discovery of Witchcraft: 45
Watching the apocalypse 61
The Rite to Roam 70
The Three Schools of Magick –
by Way of Introduction 82
Baphomet Rising 89
The Mass of Abraxas 95
The Ketacean Kundalini Kult 99
The Pope & The Prophet 110
They Rise 113
Beyond the Pharmakon 124
Return to Chaos 135
A Crisis of Chaos 141
The Black Flag & The Mystery 146
The Gratuitous Grace 152
Lessons from the Witches 153
Wine & Strange Drugs 159
New Age Zombie Apocalypse 167
Chaos Buddha Rite 174
Intensify the Normal 177
Sources 178
Notes, bibliography 179

For all those who have been in crisis

Deep Magic Begins Here...

This book continues my confession. That's what much of my writing really is. The material presented in this book continues the tales that I told, both directly and indirectly in *Magick Works*. In that volume, published in 2005, I had opened up something of a personal spiritual abyss. Although I'd fondly imagined I'd crossed the worst of it back then, the most difficult part of the trip was yet to come.

This volume then consists predominantly of writings that I'd produced during an intense period of emotional upheaval. The breakdown of a long-term relationship with my then partner, the experience of moving out, reduced contact with my children, legal, financial and health problems. You may well know the score. Of course one might imagine that bad things aren't supposed to happen to magicians. After all if magick is about power, then why not simply do a spell and sort the bloody mess out? I suspect that anyone reading this who knows about magick, *real* magick, not the Harry Potter fantasy of magick, will know this isn't really an option. Magick, as a number of essays in this book explore, is as much a test as it is a gift.

So in many ways this is a dark book. Its sound track has been sobbing and flashcore industrial music, long silent periods and Godspeed You Black Emperor. But at least, though magick may initiate or at least attend such life changes, the traditions teach us (to quote Bill Hicks, Peace be Upon Him) that 'it's just a ride'; we are riders on The Wheel of Fortune. One day we are on the up, rising high and living our dreams, then we are cast downward, yet still we may rise again.

I'd like to thank the wide range of lovely people with whom I have been in touch through this time. Especially Nick, Nikki, P., Greg and most especially Steve without whose ministry I may well have gone mad in an even more debilitating way. I offer love to all the members of my family, to my good friends in the various Pagan traditions I have been honoured to encounter, and to my dear colleagues of the Illuminates of Thanateros.

This collection begins where my previous solo book *Magick Works* ends, with me literally hanging from an ancient yew tree.

Come with me now, into the darkness…

The Pain of Division

> Midway upon the journey of our life
> I found myself within a forest dark,
> For the straightforward pathway had been lost.
> Ah me! How hard a thing it is to say
> What was this forest savage, rough, and stern,
> Which in the very thought renews the fear.
>
> Dante, *The Divine Comedy.*

Back at home and sitting in the garden. My chest is a little sore but otherwise there seem to be no ill effects. So what happened? If I think back I recall most vividly the images – my chest bare, lying down in the corpse asana, looking up through the limbs of the yew, at the slowly fading light. I am relaxed, lying like the immobile Shiva. My hands are palms up, opening, receiving. My skin, after the confinement of winter, seems very white or perhaps I'm glowing slightly, a faint ghostly blue light. Q. comes over; his rangy form moving easily and deliberately above me. I'm the first to be pierced (of seven people, having chosen lots from my top hat). He kneels beside me and I hear the rustling of his bag. There is the unmistakable sound of medical grade plastic ripping. He doesn't take long, the needle is out and ready. Though I don't see this I know what he is up to, the 4mm shaft is prepared. Here we go.

What is The Tower, what does this omen mean? Destruction; the bolt from the blue, the opening of the mouth, devouring. I remember being at the top of The Wheel. I thought I was living my dream. Truly pride goeth before a fall. My family, my home, my lover, my work, my community. All these things, these glorious attachments. The Tower reminds us that all these things can disappear from us, from me.

The Tower reminds us of the impermanence of things. How our most cherished creations can come crashing down. So when we ritualise and bring our attention to Atu XVI we can find ourselves plunged like those tiny figures. Launched into the uncertain sky, falling earthward, uprooted and screaming from the purchase of that which we knew. Do we, as magicians, invoke these things onto ourselves or does our practice merely reflect the natural processes of our humanity through the lens of what we call magick?

My own crisis developed out of a ritual in an ancient yew forest in Sussex. A ritual where my flesh would be attached to a venerable tree. The ceremony was to be a powerful one. But it was the act of being cut down, of my impaled flesh being released from the tree, which would make the difference.

P. has already briefed us about the probable order of ceremony for the piercing. "Take three good slow breaths, at the end of the third exhalation the needle will go through". Q. disregards this rubric; "breath in", he says, and as I inhale I feel pressure on the skin he has clamped over my right breast, just above the nipple and slightly towards my midline. My body shivers slightly. I've put myself into the most relaxed state I can attain but still a quiver rises up through from my spinal nerve and I see my left foot twitch. He says, "Well done, that's the first one in". Then the same rustling of the bag and in a moment Q. is at my head, squatting near my left shoulder. "Breath in…". This one seems to take fractionally longer to push through the skin and subcutaneous fat. It is every so slightly more painful, that is if 'pain' is the right word. It's a deep, blunt sensation, more like having a shit than getting sliced by a knife. The sensation is the deep bass note of serious injury, not the high treble of a paper cut.

When we do ritual we always throw ourselves into space, into the Mystery. Where will we fall? What will the ceremony do? However detailed our preparations, however thorough our knowledge of the grimoires or the gnosis, there is always that unknown. And that is why 'to Dare' is one of the powers of the magician.

As magicians we are also used to building up our worlds. This autopoiesis, a self-creation through the Will. But there are times when that pesky True Will, our daemon, has ideas of its own. What I want, what might be comfortable and convenient, may not be what the True Will desires. And when the True Will rises up against the velvet lined fortresses we have made for ourselves, then the crash comes. The Tower haunts our divinations. Reminds us of the necessity of the Solve *as well as* Coagula.

Now both hooks are in and P. comes to me. "Well done Frater," he says. I begin to sit; I feel pretty normal yet have just voluntarily undergone this weird act. There are bloody enormous (or so they seem) bits of metal attached through me. Unlike taking a psychedelic (where we do something normal, for example eating a plant, and end up in a radically different state of consciousness) this is doing something quite bizarre and yet being left quite sober and sane. I guess that is one of the points of this kind of process – which is about sobriety – yes there is the effect of the adrenaline and endogenous opiates but these give the feeling (the illusion?) that you're straight. I could get pierced in this way and then drive (at least that's how I feel, but perhaps it would not be advisable to test this). Things aren't weird in a trance way like being on drugs, which makes sense. The body kicks out all manner of glandular secretions when there is a physical assault to it. Cells scream and blood factors are marshalled, swarming to the site of the injury to prevent infection and promote healing. But whatever effect these reactions have it is important that the brain, the mind, remains clear. If a tiger has bitten you, you need to be sober enough to run away and hide. You may even need to be clear-headed and coordinated enough to fight back. So this is a lucidity trip.

Of course we know The Tower will get us at some point. Especially if, as David Beth puts it, we walk the 'merciless path'. A path where magick is our first love and that includes the horrors that it can bring as well as the joys. Magick is certainly about control and focus but it is also about embracing (or trying the embrace) the vacuum when we fall. There are times, initiations we call them, when we need to relinquish our sense of self. When we need to breakdown, to go mad. The great mage is reduced to a crying weakling, rocking back and forth like a caged animal, broken. Sure we all know the story; you've gotta do your turn in the wilderness, long haired and crazy like Nebuchadnezzar. It might take days, weeks, months, years, but we all have to go to the desert and be left alone.

P. has hoodwinked my head and tenderly wrapped my coat and open fronted robe around my shoulders. I ask (from the near darkness of the hood, now sitting up) for my rattle, P. offers this to me and I start the basic Native American style trance rhythm, quite fast. I need to externalise the shivers I feel, presumably the result of my adrenal system gearing up, getting me energised to flee or fight. With the hood still on I can hear the other participants as they stand as I did before, leaning on the yew tree being flogged. The flogging opens up the skin on the back, allowing the corresponding skin on the chest to open to the piercing.

"Would you like to stand Doctor Vayne?" asks P., I get up and he pulls my robe around me. I keep the rattle going, I've been experimenting a little with singing (the Uruz rune) while I'm hoodwinked but it's not quite right. I need to wait for the sound to arise naturally. P. pops my ritual 'Priest hat' on my head; the fox tail attached to it hangs down my back. With the hoodwink removed I can again see these big metal things hanging off me. A momentary sense of "what the fuck have I done to myself" passes through my mind. (Other thoughts; I'm like a cyborg, what if I stay like this? what if they (the ritual leaders) just go and leave me? Should I stay like this and not get attached to the tree?) P. finds the cord that runs from one hook, loops it through the rope that encircles the tree and back to the second hook. Now there is a triangle of green cord, it runs from one hook to the tree and back. The rope around the yew is thick and white. I can see the green cord, where it intersects with the rope, lights from our lanterns at the periphery of my vision. This is real, really REAL, like labour. Every detail is very, very clear.

Course It's times like that you need to pull out all the stops. Try your best to stay with your core practices. Keep your body going so your psyche can weather the storm. Fresh fruit and yoga (or if you can't manage that, fags and booze) is the way forward.

Not much point in doing divination now. Best leave that and instead try talking. Speaking to friends, allies and internal dialogues (you'll be swimming in these anyhow). Open to the emotions – grief, loss, hatred. Don't judge them or yourself. This is just the process. If your world is crashing into war allow yourself your feelings. Open to them as they are, in their own terms, as real expressions of yourself, your journey.

Of course a certain amount of flailing around (like a fish speared on a trident) is perhaps inevitable. Harsh words, ill-conceived letters and emails. Meetings that you hope might bring reconciliation become hollow dates. As a magician we want to control, to manipulate and to intervene. Why can't I just sort this sorry mess out? Do a ritual, make a decision? Why can't I see my way? It used to be all so clear.

I'm moving now, slightly, shifting my weight until I find I can get an even tension on both hooks. My brain isn't dialoguing very much with itself. This decision, to adopt a certain stance, in order to begin to pull at the hooks, is arrived at with a clear head, immediately. It reminds me of a refrain (but only on reflection) of the Current 93 song *LAShTAL* "there is nothing, there is nothing but this". I'm dancing (after a fashion) pulling on the hooks, keeping the cord that runs from my body to the tree taught. I figure (again in this curiously rational, single pointed way) that moving will allow me to get deeper into the zone and also help reduce any pain. When I was hoodwinked and kneeling I kept moving, deliberately rocking so the hooks clanked and thumped against my chest. Again this is a kind of body wisdom. I know that I want to move in much the same way that a pregnant mother knows how to move when her baby comes.

I'm looking down and can see the strain on my chest, the flesh being pulled away. A couple of inches of stretch, no blood and not exactly painful, once more the sensation is that of deep rooted pressure, a tugging as my body moves into a new shape.

My rattle is still going. I'm making sounds as well, 'hee, hah, heeee, haaah', alternating and playing with these two basic noises. These are the sounds I need to make. I'd had all kinds of ideas about singing the Futhark but these sounds I'm making now, these are the right runes to be singing.

The Tower is the heart and someday your heart might just break. You might even break your own heart, or the heart of those you love, with your magick. Imagine that. Something so rich and powerful causing such distress and fear. That's not mentioned much in all those lovely Spellcraft 101 books, you'd be forgiven for thinking that for the magician nothing goes wrong.

To my left M. is also pierced, he is singing, talking, his hands outstretched, sometimes laughing. Beside him N. has his arms out, I can see the skin pulling up from his breast. P. and K. are on the other side of the tree as is M.B who is dressed in full motley! Beside me, to my right is O. (the last to be pierced and the only person bar P. and K. who I'd met before).

We are together and yet very much in our own spaces. We gelled briefly as a group in the car park outside Kingley Vale, waiting for Q. to turn up. We'd piled in and out of the black van as Beltane showers swept over us and were replaced with bright skies. But we're all in our own spaces (though I kept my rattle and chanting going throughout the ritual and some of the other participants said this was helpful). I find I don't mind this sensation, the pulling, and I experiment with leaning back, allowing the flesh hooks to take my weight, rocking back on my heels, raising my arms and opening, opening, opening.

But there they all are. The sorry parade of great Adepts from the past. Impoverished, addicted, insane. Whether sticking that hypodermic into their veins to relieve their asthma and messianic failure. Whether impecunious and smothered with stray cats, sleeping the deep repose of the drunkard, surrounded by paintings of the witches sabbath.

Is this really the vision we want? Is this really what I signed up to? Being ostracised, tried and found wanting by the people whose respect I most crave? It's cold comfort when you're in that state, when you're falling into the Abyss, to consider it a great initiation. Sure we all know the folk wisdom; 'it's always darkest before the dawn'. 'there is a budding 'morrow in midnight', 'you can't make an omelette without breaking eggs'.

Finally the sound of moans, chanting, groans and other rattles begins to soften and die away. There had been curious echoes when the sound was at its height. Waves of noise bouncing back from the yew boughs behind me (the tree spreads out and down, enclosing us like a living cave. I estimate the tree to be 1200 years old and some 4m in diameter.) This sound effect is the only thing that I would describe as a hallucination – the sense that behind me there are other people playing rattles. I know it's just the echo but there is a feeling that it is the presence of other participants, just outside our circle who are making those sounds. Certainly there is a heightened perception, perhaps heightened awareness of possible threats ('it's behind you!'). Maybe it's the spirit of all those other warriors who have done this. Their ghosts supporting us in our venture.

We have all entered The Tower. As incarnated creatures we become fixated on our being *and frequently forget our* doing. *We are in fact a series of waves. Chemical reactions, the ebb and flow of substances, the microscopic pumping of our cells. We are matter in motion, millions upon millions of interactions moving through space-time. We call ourselves 'I', sovereign individuals. Yet the reality is that we are waves of awareness and as the wave curls over it comes crashing down.*

Now I've done. I finish my dance and rattling and, ending my chant, step forward. I touch the ancient yew tree; the bark is full of sensation and detail. The sap that glistens on the trunk in the candlelight is red.

Q. goes round and removes the hooks. I lay down to have mine slipped out and a gauze pad is pressed over the wounds to keep the holes clean. I really don't feel any pain, just that same curious interior sensation of tugging. I dress. A few more layers against the cold of the night. We're all free. People are talking, we're sharing chocolate and tea, water, spliffs. We're able to relax and laugh. Mike and O. both have impressive (but not unduly worrying) loss of blood at the sites of the puncture wounds. Nothing problematic, in fact quite cool looking.

Later that night O. and I are driving back to Brighton. I'm quite safe to drive now, no disturbance to that skill.

We're both astonished. This was a classic initiatory experience in that neither of us had imagined the aftermath of the rite. We'd been so focused on the ceremony, the unknown, of the fear and pain – what might happen. Now it was all over, in a sense the world was new, unstructured. We'd crossed the threshold of fear and passed through. The personal eschaton of the sundance had arrived and passed – we'd survived. Now was the first day of the rest of our lives, defences down, we'd not imagined this time and were naked, without a script, just here in the car travelling back to Brighton.

In each of our bags, two hooks and one fuck off big needle.

Months later I am beginning to emerge from the twisted wreckage. Slowly the sound of universes crashing into war dulls to a distant rumble. After Atu XVI what comes next? At midnight, standing outside the peyote circle, I reach upwards towards

The Star.

The Sabbat of Chaos

A deep voice begins the invocation:

> O mighty Rehctaw! Thou who exists in all erogenousness, We evoke Thee!
>
> By the power of the meanings arising from these forms I make. We evoke Thee!
>
> By the Talismans that speak the secret leitmotif of desire, We evoke Thee!
>
> By the sacrifices, abstinences and transvaluations we make, We evoke Thee!
>
> By the sacred inbetweeness concepts Give us the flesh!
>
> By the quadriga sexualis Give us unvarying desire!
>
> By the conquest of fatigue Give us eternal resurgence!
>
> By the most sacred Word-graph of Heaven We invoke Thee!

Two participants are dressed in their Halloween finery, leather corsets, high heels and pointy hats. One of them carries a jar containing a green substance, flying ointment.

Anointed with this magical unguent our participants sit in silence. A soundtrack begins, the rapid drumming lulling them into the trance.

The sound of the wind fills the temple, then the half heard moans of ecstasy and of pain. The participants are flying over the inner world landscape. Caught in the wind they rise up into the heavens and looking down on the bare tops of the mountains they can see the place of the witch's sabbat. Then comes the chant, "Isis, Astarte, Athena, Hekate…" and with the twangling of instruments the sound of rave music fills the air. They arrive in the hurly burly of the imagined sabbatic feast. What first appears as a horrific parody of the Christian Mass is revealed to be a naked celebration of joyous life.

And as the dance comes to an end so they return to this world. And the spell is sealed with the words of Doreen Valiente:

> "Oh, I have been beyond the town,
>
> Where nightshade black and mandrake grow,
>
> and I have heard and I have seen
>
> What righteous folk would fear to know!
>
> ...
>
> Oh, I have been and I have seen,
>
> In magick worlds of Otherwhere.
>
> For all this world may praise or blame,
>
> For ban or blessing nought I care.
>
> For I have been beyond the town,
>
> Where meadowsweet and roses grow,
>
> And there such music did I hear
>
> As worldly-righteous never know."

And the ritual is banished with cackling.

As a chaos magician I'm always interested in rituals, in methods for changing consciousness. So what does this brief excerpt from a recent chaos magick ritual that I created tell us about the chaos approach?

The first point is that chaos magick isn't, as is sometimes claimed, a style that necessarily tends towards the superficial. A typical chaos magick meeting often involves a 'bring and share' model, where participants bring a ritual practice or exercise to share with others. This means that participants can experience a method that is the distillation of the long-term practice of the person presenting the ritual.

The ceremony above was the climax of a long period of personal work and is rooted in the fact that I've been personally involved in the style of magick known as witchcraft for over twenty-five years. However this isn't a 'classic' Wiccan Book of Shadows sabbat. Instead it's one, which happily draws its inspiration from a multiplicity of sources.

The invocation, for example, is from the sabbatic ritual created by Austin Osman Spare who is perhaps the single most important influence on chaos magick. Austin Spare was a genius, one of the greatest nude portrait artists of his time (so said the newspapers on the occasion of his death in 1956). Spare combined his formidable artist talents with his own intensely personal system of sorcery that included the technique of sigilisation which is perhaps his best known legacy.

The witches officiating at the ceremony were dressed as, well, witches. If you ask a passer-by to describe a witch they might tell you she (and it is almost invariably a she rather than he) is a loathsome hag or else a desirable harlot. Her gothic style clothing is marked with the silver traces of spiders' webs and, of course, she wears a witch's hat. By making conscious use of this image the ritual plugs directly into our mythology as it exists now, and this is a key feature of chaos magick. Although chaos magicians certainly do work with 'traditional' deities they are equally happy in using our lexicon of current cultural symbols. This can mean that plenty of chaos rituals might look like psychotherapeutic practices since psychology is a powerful modern retelling of how magick works. Equally a chaos magician might decide to do ritual involving characters from film culture, contemporary literature, or recent history.

Then there is the flying ointment. Of course in the exploration of our consciousnesses there are many occasions when magicians and Pagans of many traditions make use of 'plant teachers', particularly those substances that are frequently referred to as psychedelics. However anyone who knows about this territory will tell you that the 'traditional' drugs that make up flying ointment (belladonna, aconite, henbane, datura etc) are basically a recipe for disaster. Rather than risk killing anyone at my ritual I therefore decided to instead go for toothpaste mixed with green food colouring. Smeared on the body this potion would cause a tingling sensation but nothing more. The power here was in belief (the role of belief is of major importance as the 'frame' within which magick operates in the chaos style). I'd told the participants that this was flying ointment, that it did have homeopathic traces of the traditional ingredients present (it didn't) and that they should trust me! As a chaos magician I believe that much of what makes magick work is our belief in it. The placebo effect is one such example of this process and so the very idea that this was flying ointment is itself magickal.

(Obviously this is also a comment that, when working with wildly different systems and methods participants need to have a high degree of experience in occultism and feel confident in trusting their Brothers and Sisters.)

There is the use of modern technology. The music I'd prepared for this ritual (which you can find if you look me up on vimeo.com) was created using a simple freeware sound-editing package. By layering sounds (including trance drumming, sounds sampled from hard-core sadomasochistic pornography, the Lord's Prayer said backwards and so forth) a complex soundscape can be produced. Chaos magicians, while very happy to do 'empty handed magick' (that is magick which requires no ritual props at all) are typically quite willing to deploy multimedia systems, biofeedback and other technological aids in their rituals.

The ritual pivots on various ways of changing consciousness since, for chaos magicians, this is one of the core issues of magickal praxis. Generating 'gnosis' or an altered state happens in this rite through ritual poetry, through the placebo flying ointment, through visualisation and motionlessness and, once the music kicks in, through trance dance.

After the sabbatic journey the rite concludes with the wonderful ritual poetry of Doreen Valiente. Once again this is an example of me bringing my tradition (witchcraft) to share with my colleagues. This is a poem which I first encountered in my teens and which beautifully summarises the ritual. Namely that 'the sabbat' appears to be, at first, all about darkness and death ("where nightshade black and mandrake grow") but resolves itself into joy and an affirmation of life ("where meadowsweet and roses grow"). The poem also affirms the simple fact that being a magician often means going against the grain ("for all this world may praise or blame, for ban or blessing naught I care"). Chaos magicians recognise that while we live in communities and work for good relationships with others, the path of magick is a challenging one, both personally and socially. Magicians (of whatever tradition) seek to change the universe both inner and outer; to rock the boat of the status quo. The motto of the chaos magician is perhaps best summarised by the famous dictum of Timothy Leary (himself a Brother of the chaos magick order I am a member of) "Think for yourself and question authority".

The final act of the ritual is to banish the space, to open the circle if you will. This is traditionally done in chaos magick with laughter. Laughing helps break the mood of the rite. It helps us forget our intention (and therefore allow it to sink into the unconscious, deep mind to gestate). Moreover it reminds us not to be too serious about our magick. We should hold our beliefs in magick, and our view of ourselves as magicians, with both great seriousness and also generous humour. 'Mirth and Reverence' as it says in the Wiccan Charge of The Goddess. And of course what better way to end a Samhain ritual but to transform that laughter into the cackling giggles of the Crone?

So there's a practical example chaos magick in action. Of course other rituals and programmes will inevitably look very different but many of the core elements will remain the same. If you want to find out more the Internet is a rich resource. Iot.org.uk will also point you towards actively working chaos magicians in both the British Isles and globally. As far as books are concerned naturally I'd recommend my own, those of P. Carroll and of course Terry Pratchett. You may also wish to investigate arcamoriumcollege.com where a number of chaos-influenced magicians teach courses on many different aspects of the occult arts.

So, as we say in my tradition "Choyofaque!" which means, "Do the Great Work of Magick" and as they also say in my tradition "Blessed Be".

Mastering Witchcraft

WEEK 1

Out of the moonlit night it comes. The cool breath of the wind through the darkness. It carries the sounds from long ago, from ancient lands. It speaks of hidden chambers, of twisted trees on desolate moorland. It speaks of deep magick.

Outside the circle of firelight we call civilisation, strange forces prowl. Spirits and watchers from elder times. It is into this darkness that we will step, and there we shall make our enchantments. We shall slip through the cracks in reality, arriving at a world between that of men and of Gods. In these secret spaces we shall brew our spells, acts of transformation that will fill us with pleasure and freedom and power.

Witchcraft means many things. For some it is the Masonic mystery religion psychodrama of the Alexandrian style of Wicca. For others it is hedge witchcraft; practised in kitchens that enchant the everyday world. For some it is the look of wildness in the eyes of an animal. For others it is the establishment of the magickal dream within the tradition of the Cultus Sabbati.

Personally I'm less interested in witchcraft as a specific thing, a given tradition or praxis. Rather it is a style, a way of imagining the occult that revels in the mysterious aspects of magick. This style is not necessarily antithetical to the quasi-scientific approaches of chaos magick. But it is one in which we have a wide variety of symbols, common cultural memes, which we can use like the rungs of a ladder to climb down into the chamber of our 'deep mind'.

The 'deep mind', according to Paul Huson, who wrote his gem of a text *Mastering Witchcraft* in 1970, is that shadowy realm of the unconscious from which our magical powers issue. And implicit within the style of calling it the deep mind (rather than 'unconscious') is Huson's observation; "Nothing so arouses the deep mind's attention in anyone than the call of the dark, arcane, and mysterious."

One thing that differentiates a child's game of make-believe from a genuine witch's magical operation is that vital occult factor of the deep mind's part in the work. Unless that underlying stratum of psychical coexistence here designated as the deep mind is penetrated, the 'magick' remains totally within the personal sphere of the operator, at best remaining an exercise of surface autosuggestion; at worst, a fantasy refuge from a hostile outside world. Only when the 'deeps' are contacted, only at that point does any real witchcraft take place.

So let's imagine a witchcraft, which is an aeon's deep magick. The kind of magick you find in dusty books hidden in remote ruined castles, the kind that is so ordinary that it is done with jam jars and pins. The kind that reaches back into atavistic memory but is able to fly to the stars.

Through this course we will work with the Four Powers of the Witches Pyramid, again described by Huson (and you would do well to buy a copy of his classic work). These are also known as the four powers of the magician.

But before we meet the pyramid our course begins with a simple ritual and the study of a legend, perhaps *the* legend, of the witches.

Arrange a solitary space with subdued lighting, burn some incense, and read the following invocation, which is known as The Charge of the Goddess, aloud.

> Listen to the words of the Great Mother;
>
> she who of old was also called among men
>
> Artemis, Astarte, Athene, Dione, Melusine,
>
> Aphrodite, Cerridwen, Cybele, Arianrhod,
>
> Isis, Dana, Bride
>
> and by many other names:
>
> Whenever ye have need of anything,
>
> once in the month, and better it be when the moon is full,
>
> then shall ye assemble in some secret place
>
> and adore the spirit of me,

who am Queen of all the witches.

There shall ye assemble,

ye who are fain to learn all sorcery,

yet have not won its deepest secrets;

to these will I teach things that are yet unknown.

And ye shall be free from slavery;

and as a sign that ye be really free,

ye shall be naked in your rites;

and ye shall dance, sing, feast,

make music and love,

all in my praise.

For mine is the ecstasy of the spirit,

and mine also is joy on earth;

for my law is love unto all beings.

Keep pure your highest ideal;

strive ever towards it;

let naught stop you or turn you aside.

For mine is the secret door

which opens upon the Land of Youth,

and mine is the cup of the wine of life,

and the Cauldron of Cerridwen,

which is the Holy Grail of immortality.

I am the Gracious Goddess,

who gives the gift of joy unto the heart of man.

Upon earth, I give the knowledge of the spirit eternal;

and beyond death, I give peace and freedom

and reunion with those who have gone before.

Nor do I demand aught in sacrifice;

for behold,

I am the Mother of all living,

and my love is poured out upon the earth.

Hear ye the words of the Star Goddess;

she in the dust of whose feet are the hosts of heaven,

and whose body encircles the universe.

I who am the beauty of the green earth,

and the white Moon among the stars,

and the mystery of the waters,

and the desire of the heart of man,

call unto thy soul.

Arise, and come unto me.

For I am the soul of nature, who gives life to the universe.

From me all things proceed,

and unto me all things must return;

and before my face, beloved of Gods and of men,

let thine innermost divine self be enfolded in the rapture of the infinite.

Let my worship be within the heart that rejoiceth;

for behold,

all acts of love and pleasure are my rituals.

And therefore let there be beauty and strength,

power and compassion, honour and humility,

mirth and reverence within you.

And thou who thinkest to seek for me,

know thy seeking and yearning shall avail thee not

unless thou knowest the mystery;

that if that which thou seekest

thee findest not within thee,

thou wilt never find it without thee.

For behold,

I have been with thee from the beginning;

and I am that which is attained

at the end of desire.

The next process is for you to read and perform the ceremony given below. Read the ritual, do it this week and then report your findings (by creating your own journal thread).

The door is open to the witch's cottage. Will you step in and meet her? Perhaps you could even become her?

Initiation

This ritual of self-initiation as given by Huson in *Mastering Witchcraft*. It should be done on three consecutive nights. You must ensure that you will not be disturbed. The core of the rite is very simple but feel free to elaborate on it (for example by using a banishing or circle casting rite) if that seems appropriate for you. The best time for this ritual is midnight.

Light a single candle and repeat over it the following words. If you cannot memorise them you should write (not print) them out.

NEMA! LIVEE, MORF SU REVILLED TUB NOISHAYTPMET OOTNI TON SUH DEEL SUS TSHAIGA SAPSERT TAHT YETH. VIGRAWF EU ZA SESAPSERT RUA SUH VIGRAWF DERB ILAID RUA YED SITH SUH VIG NEVEH NI SI ZA THRE NI NUD EEB LIW EYTH MUCK MODNGIK EYTH MAIN EYTH EEB DWOHLAH NEVAH NI TRA CHIOO. RETHARF RUA!

NOTE: Text is written phonetically.

Huson writes
"*As you chant the words, use your imagination to visualise great iron shackles struck*

off your hands and feet by sizzling bolts of lightning and disintegrating into molten shards to either side of you. Hear the whine and crackle of the searing flashes as they accomplish the work of liberation, and consciously try to feel the burden of all your inherited guilts, all those awful shalt's and shalt not's, all that vast edifice of twaddle and claptrap, sliding easefully from your back.

When all is over, blow out the candle, uttering the witch words "So mote it be!" Should you feel any frissons of fear creeping up your spine during the performance of what may appear to you palpable blasphemy, it is all to the good. This is a process of purgation and catharsis and often carries with it a certain echo of childhood fears. Don't worry, though; any cold shivers only herald the fact that your deep mind is sitting up and taking notice. It is through your deep mind that you will develop your powers once you have cleared away the litter and debris that usually clogs it, as indeed is generally the case of the ordinary man-in-the-street.

Each of the three successive days when you get up in the morning, you must strive to remember who you are, a witch, what you did the night before, and the reason you did it. Then, maintaining that same frame of mind, embark upon the coming day.

Strictly speaking, this 'unravelling' is only necessary as a gesture for the first three nights to mark your initial step on the path.

Anyway, the feeling of release that should accompany this little rite is a sure indication that the way is open for the powers to begin flowing within you. It is as simple as that. No risky copulation with fellow initiates on top of damp tombstones. No messy crucifixion of toads. Just a simple loosening of the mundane knot—a process of blessed unbinding."

To check the pronunciation you may wish to record your voice and reverse the waveform in a sound editing computer application.

A Note on Blasphemy
One might well object that the act of reciting the Pater Noster backwards isn't very transgressive these days. My answer to this firstly that it depends a lot on where you live and with whom. We live in a time in history when the 'slave God' religions still exert tremendous power. Europe has its own theocratic state in the Vatican and even a deeply secular nation like the British Isles still has Christian ministers sitting, by

right, in its legislature. Secondly if you really don't think what might seem like a rather juvenile satanic ceremony will do the business for you, then write your own. Consider what it would be blasphemous to say (forward or backwards!) in this age and this culture. There are, to mix our religious metaphors, still plenty of sacred cows contentedly grazing in the noosphere.

WEEK 2

Over the course of the next four weeks we shall be working with what Huson calls "...that most important of subjects, that dark tower of sorcery itself, the witches' pyramid."

Written on the four cornerstones of the pyramid are the four powers of the witch; imagination, will, faith and secrecy. These are the four arts that we shall cultivate during the coming month.

During this time we shall also be paying attention to the natural rhythms of magick as they flow from the earth, the sun, the moon and the stars. By paying attention to these tides we will know the best times to launch our sorcery. This practice is also essential for forming a magickal link between the inner psychic realm of the witch and the outer world of manifestation. Spend some time looking into the planetary hour systems. Many methods of calculating planetary hours are to be found in old school occult books from the 1980s and on the Internet.

The virulent imagination that the witch should cultivate should manifest itself in many ways. Paul Huson explains how this may appear in one's choice of interior decor;

"This, of course, is the rationale behind the traditional trappings of witchcraft—quite apart from the paraphysical implications of the rituals. A suitable setting for your magical acts is therefore requisite as one of the primary stimulants to your witchy imagination. A living room or den is about the best most of us can manage in these days, but this is where your imagination comes in and invests the place of working with all the mystery and terror sufficient to start your black juices flowing. The occasional grotesque statuette or bizarre print is all to the good. In fact, as a witch, you will be obliged to collect around yourself over the course of time a good complement of sorcerers' trinkets. They don't necessarily have to be the genuine articles—real skulls and goat's-foot candlesticks are hard to come by and somewhat expensive—

but seeing that atmosphere is so important, it is worth investing in the odd dime-store Pacific Island devil mask or reproduction of a medieval astrological chart. It will probably grow to be a passion with you as time passes, and you may soon find yourself having to resist sternly the lure of any junk or antique shop you happen to pass, purely in the interests of economy.

So treasure up your fantasies. The controlled daydream is one of the main keys to being a successful witch. In fact, dream on, the richer and more fantastic the better!"

So this week I'd like you to go and find yourself something suitably arcane looking to have in your home. Of course some of you will already have homes protected from the evil eye by conspicuous witch-balls and be walking around a virtual chandelier of lucky whalebones and pixie teeth! But wherever you can add a little more of the witchy sensibility do so this week. Please try to upload a photo of your new acquisition. This could be something as small as an item of jewellery or as large as you like.

Once you've found your object do the following ritual to imbue it with witchpower.

Consecration

Consider the times and seasons, the clock time, the phase of the moon and the planetary hours and determine when it is best to do this ritual. Search books and on-line to find out more about the various systems that exist and choose one that makes sense (but not necessarily the most convenient!).

Consecration is an excellent example of a magical process that majors in the use of the imagination. The aim is to mark your new possession off as something special, in a sense reserved from the everyday world by dint of its distinctive connection with the realm of magick. It can most easily be imagined as filling the object up with magical power.

Begin by drawing a magick circle in your working space. If you already possess wands, athames and all the rest use them, if not just your index finger will do. Visualise the circle being composed of blue flame (think of how brandy or methylated spirit burn, that's the kind of colour you're after). The 'circle' could actually be a cone of power, a sphere or a column of protected space if it seems peculiar to only use a 2D figure. The circle is generally cast deosil. If you need any more hints about how to go about it please look on-line.

Once the circle is formed place your witchy object in the centre and fill it with power. You might choose just to use visualisation (perhaps jets of blue flame emanating from your palms and bathing your object) or words, or some other technique. The point here is to imagine what would do the job. Make the ceremony as elaborate or simple as you like. Once you have filled your object with power close (or 'open') your circle by your preferred method. The simplest method is to reverse your steps with a widdershins motion imagining the circle power fading and vanishing.

Post your results.

WEEK 3

This week we shall be working with the element of will.

Huson writes:
"The second side of the witches' pyramid of power is firmly labelled "wil"l. It almost goes without saying that the establishment of a potent will is one of the main goals of a practitioner of the Black Arts. The will in this instance is a magical one, however, and if viewed out of magical context and within the framework of everyday life, would constitute a splendid example of extravagant egocentricity or even megalomania. It is the will of a spoiled child we are dealing with here, one that brooks no opposition and impudently stares down any attempt at resistance with a basilisk eye.

This will is switched on during the actual magical operation, and it functions hand in hand with the bubbling and boiling emotions evoked by means of your wicked imagination. It is in effect the lens through which the burning emotions are focused. In order to sharpen your will to the correct needlepoint, you may wish to employ one or two aids in the form of simple exercises designed to help concentration. Eastern disciplines such as certain yoga meditation exercises can be used. They are very wearisome, but they do work, with perseverance.

Meditating on the single flame of a candle is also good, as is keeping the attention fixed upon a painted dot within a circle for half an hour without budging. The attempt to gaze at the second hand of a watch completing the circuit of one minute, maintaining one's awareness of the hand at every second is also very rewarding, and is frequently used by witches as a toning-up exercise for the will, here used to direct the attention."

So taking Mr Huson's advice to heart, this week is going to be about candle meditation. Find a time and place where you will not be disturbed. Take a pin and place it in the candle a little way down the shaft. You may want to experiment with the type of candle you have chosen to determine how rapidly it burns. Place the pin in the candle and bring your will to focus on the flame. Stay with this practice until the pin drops out, 'let naught stop you or turn you aside'.

This method is an excellent technique for casting spells – when the pin falls you release the energy and the spell goes to work. In this case the spell is implicit in your commitment to stay with the process until the pin falls; you are tempering your will.

Do this at least twice this week and record your results. Those who have access to the Wii Fit Zazen program may do the physical candle once and then the console game instead!

Again consider when you do this practice and at which planetary hour you are working.

WEEK 4

Faith is the next cornerstone of the witches pyramid. Paul Huson has the following to say on this subject:

"Unless you possess a rock-firm faith in your own powers and in the operability of your spell, you will not achieve the burning intensity of will and imagination which is requisite to make the magick work.

Faith is the vice in which you hold steady your crucible will, into which you pour the molten metal of your virulent imagination. If you reflect on it, you will see in effect that imagination and faith are both very intimately connected with the will. Faith is that which sweeps away all remaining objections and clears the decks for immediate action. It is one of those valuable props, which support you temporarily, in the course of your magical operation, and allow you to believe in the inevitability of the success, which is bound to be attendant upon it. It is one more means of attaining that special state of self-imposed and hopefully temporary megalomania that is the sine qua non of all true acts of sorcery.

You must be well aware of the great part faith plays in the dealings of those individuals who wrestle with the more arcane aspects of fate in one way or another. A spiritual healer or a master gambler would no more approach a prospective patient or crap game cold, without the flame of faith in their powers to warm them, than would a microscopist approach his specimen without a microscope. At a rudimentary level, if you didn't have the faith you could do it, you could no more put one foot before the other and cross the road in the manner you do every day, than could a two-month-old baby. In magical matter, faith is de rigueur, and due to this fact it merits a whole side of the witches' pyramid to itself."

Faith, especially in the modern world, can sometimes feel a bit odd. We confuse it with blind, foolhardy or fundamentalist beliefs. But faith in oneself and the effectiveness of one's process is essential. In chaos magick we might talk about 'belief shifting' but 'belief sticking', entering and staying with a paradigm for as long as is necessary, also matters.

In order to make faith 'rock-firm' it needs to seem natural and easy, self-evident and sure. So this week I'd like you to explain how a magick spell works. Don't go for some post-modernist flim-flam; explain to the best of your ability how you believe it works. If, at bottom, you think it's the action of spirits say so, if you really think it's all applied psychology then say that. If you want to use the language of the parapsychologist or physicist that's fine, but if you want to put your point across using a more artistic or evocative language do so.

Write down your explanation for how magick REALLY works and post it this week.

WEEK 5

The final power we shall touch on this week is the art of secrecy. There are several different aspects to this, ranging from being a little circumspect as to who knows what you get up to, through to the importance of letting go and allowing your spells to work 'without lust of result'.

Paul Huson writes

"...*practise dropping the occasional portentous hints about your magick, never of course being too explicit, but always striving to convey just enough to activate people's curiosities without making them too sceptical. Of course, you will have to be selective with what you say to people. Not everyone is susceptible to the same pitch. With some, after being pressed in vain to say more, you may find yourself confronted with the retort, "Well, don't tell us if you don't want to; see if we care!" But they do. And it has aroused their interests sufficiently for them to expend energy on an emotion of petulance. The worst kind of response to your engineered secrecy is one of "Oh, really ... Did I tell you about that movie I saw the other day?" So be discriminating with your portentous hints. Sum up your audience or victim before you slyly murmur in their ears.*"

Paul Huson also points out the legal issues that have surrounded magick in the past and still surround certain types of occultism (such as the use of entheogens) today.

"Another, more mundane reason for preserving a modicum of secrecy is this: Though the burning days are over, you must still keep one eye open for the law on one or two points. For instance, should one of your wax voodoo dolls be brought into court and shown as sufficient evidence of your practice of psychological intimidation upon an intended victim, you could find yourself in trouble with a lawsuit on your hands and heavy damages may be awarded against you."

This week we shall make a traditional witches talisman that is framed by secrecy.

The term 'witch bottle' has several meanings within the Craft. The variant that we are going to produce this week is a protective talisman for the witch that relies on secrecy and cunning. The process is very simple and creates an object that is analogous to a battery; a reservoir of witch power you can draw on whenever you have need of it.

The act is a sorcerous form of magick, which you can make as elaborate (or not) as you wish. The key elements of these are as follows:

1. Obtain a jar (a typical jam jar will suffice).

2.   Collect a series of sharp objects; pins, shards of glass, nails.

3.   Place these in the jar and fill it with your urine.

4.   Seal the jar and hide it.

Obviously you will want to keep your imagination, will and faith focused throughout this process. Once you seal the jar you will need to take it, ideally under cover of darkness, and hide it. Find a powerspot in your area that is suitable for this work. Typical examples of such spots are Churches, graveyards, crossroads, waterfalls, the foot of ancient trees etc.

Do not tell a soul about the details of this work, at the most you can mutter something mysterious about 'burying a talisman in the woods' but no more than that. On no account should you reveal the location of your witch bottle to another living soul. However on your thread you may simply wish to confirm that you have done this work.

Also on your thread this week please spend some time surfing the Internet, scanning from books, or uploading your own artwork. We're going to need lots of images of witches for the climax of our course next week. Please find at least two images that for you sum up the essence of witchcraft and share these on your thread.

WEEK 6

"In the circle of firelight which we are pleased to call an enlightened scientific civilisation, we usually feel secure in the knowledge that most of our worst childhood terrors and nightmares were merely fantasy. But if and when the firelight happens to dim, at those times when the unknown presses hard upon us, in the presence of death or insanity or insurmountable calamity, we again know instinctively that science is ultimately irrelevant, and we once again experience the old childhood terrors.

We are still powerless in the face of overmastering fate. Science still completely fails to come to grips with that outer darkness beyond the flickering ring of light.

However, down the ages it has seemed to some intrepid souls that only with weapons forged from the darkness itself, and by the aid of those others before them who have made it their business to know the ways in and out of the unseen world, can any man maybe hope to bend to his will an indifferent fate, whose roots appear to reach back into the outer regions of that night.

Among those who understand the darkness which is no darkness to them anymore are those that tread the way of witchcraft. They of their own accord have walked beyond the ring of firelight and learned the paths in the wilderness beyond."

So writes Paul Huson, and now we are going to claim our places as daring souls, as witches, by stepping outside of the fire lit circle and into the rich, mysterious darkness.

This week we are going to make the journey to the witches sabbat. Use of flying ointment is optional (but do be careful, mishaps with belladonna alkaloids are not unknown!). If you are unfamiliar with the typical goings on at a witches sabbat please do some investigation. Please also spend some time browsing the images of witches that have been posted to threads last week.

Choose an appropriate planetary hour (night is best but not essential if you can sufficiently darken your working room). Cast your circle using your preferred method and use the sound file posted at vimeo.com for your journey (the images are just there to get you in the mood, not necessarily for use in your actual ceremony). The first stage of the journey uses a simple drumbeat to induce a trance. You will then hear the wind and the backwards Lord's Prayer as you near the site of the sabbat. You may well feel fear as you face the imagined degeneracy and violence of the sabbatic festival but as the soundscape develops you come to see that the sabbat is in fact a celebration of joy, light and life. The track includes a piece of dance music (by 'Witchcraft'). You may feel inspired to dance in your physical body or may wish to continue to move only in your astral form. Finally there is a poem about the experience to seal the spell (by Doreen Valiente). At the end of your journey drink some wine and make a toast to the Old Ones in whatever way feels fitting. Close your circle if you have cast one or otherwise banish the space.

Listen to this inner journey at least once during this week and report on what you saw and experienced at the sabbat in your thread. Record any significant dreams during this period as well.

Dredd Lord of the Shadows

Horned One, how long have I known you? I recall your shape as a carved antelope, elongated body and spiralling horns. Discovered in a charity shop, I enshrined this statue in my bedroom between trailing ivy plants. I made offerings to you as I lost my milk teeth: enamel and blood. I called you 'Rammastaff', my secret God, inspired by Saki's murderous tale of Sredni Vashtar. You were my childish religion.

Then I created you as a mask. Papier-mache and black paint. I imagined your worshippers; we would be 'the Black Cult' and offer up wild dances and sacrifices in your name.

Your form seemed to call out at me from 2000AD - the comic that is. I recall receiving the second issue and avidly reading the strip of Judge Dredd. This 22nd century lawman did his work hidden beneath a dark visored helmet. I remember going through that first story and adding what I felt was missing from the drawings of that character; horns.

I came to know your form as Levi's sabbat goat, the icon of Karnayna depicted in esoteric picture books of intense looking Alexandrian witches. And as I read more and more of the occult cannon I found you again and again.

Halloween 1981 and I am prepared. My room is darkened and huge tapers flame in the gigantic candlesticks I've created. My *Book of Shadows* rests on the lectern, another item I crafted myself. On the altar (also hand-made) rests my athame, a chalice, and all the proper magickal paraphernalia.

I'm about to attempt my first invocation and assumption of a godform. I've read all the theory and been preparing myself with daily meditations on the attributes of my chosen deity. I've literally built the furnishings of my temple, and, importantly, arranged for my parents and sisters to be out until I've done.

The circle is cast and incense of storax and of patchouli hangs in the air.

Clouds of it rapidly fill the room, spiral up from the cast iron cauldron in which the charcoal rests. I begin my invocations to Set.

Of course Set, Seth, the Egyptian Lord of the Darkness and Chaos, doesn't have horns, but instead the ears of an unknown species (strangely square, looking rather space-age I always think). But in my mind he occupied much of the same niche as the Horned Deity of Samhain. Moreover his bisexuality appealed to both my actual predilections and theoretical understanding of the liminal gnosis.

IAO IO IA SET, SETH, SHAITAN… holding my athame I spoke the invocation and the spell began to work. From my jaws a green, smoky crystalline snout began to form, those trademark ears (or were they antlers?) sprouted from my head. I felt my body enlarge, like a frog being inflated by an errant schoolboy; my shoulders became huge corners of volcanic glass. My fingers grew long elegant nails of diamond sharpness. I was Set.

Fast forward to 1989. We are in a house in Lincolnshire, several witches, naked and dancing. It's Beltane and I am hunting, running with the herd, seeking the King Stag. The forest dances between my quarry and me. A dark haired sadhu (soon to become a leading light in the chaos magick movement, playing the part of the forest, hiding my quarry from me) expertly avoids my knife blade. But I am coming for that deer, my knife is raised again, the expectation of blood on the living room floor, but the High Priestess calls 'down!' The sadhu drops to the ground, the King Stag is still. His face is daubed ashen white and I am crowned with his antlers. Serpents are painted onto my wrists. The High Priestess and I perform The Great Rite.

Years later…I am falling, down into the earth. There is a tapestry in front of me composed of swampy greens, violets and indigo curved lights. These strobe and flood into one another, and the sound! The hissing of blood in my ears, the roaring of universes crashing into war. The sine wave of obliteration and recreation, and behind it all a growling bass note which shifts exponentially higher and higher, rising from the depths of the Underworld to the pinnacles of the heavens.

It's overwhelming. I am not I, I am All! I am unfettered consciousness.

And on the return I know that my form, my body, is the sensory organ of God, of Baphomet.

I believe that the experience of altered states of consciousness, of gnosis or trance, allow us to perceive the underlying nature of the universe, its occult patterns. In an entheogenically inspired state, for example, we begin by noticing deep structures such as breathing, the saccading of our eyes or the presence of phosphenes. We can travel, beyond this enhanced sensitivity to our physiological activity, and get down to the root of consciousness. When we see trippy fractating patterns on, say, mushrooms, we are seeing thoughts, mental processes. The movement of these forms is the basic cognitive unit. Movement is the root of self-aware living systems; an amoeba can move towards something or away from something. When we see morphing patterns on psychedelics we are seeing the relationship of thoughts expressed through geometric kinaesthesia. The consciousness of the universe is the 'thing' that collapses the all-potential chaos into discrete beings (or rather *doings* since the collapse gives rise to motion). This coming-into-being is what we see in trance. Our sense of time breaks down, the refresh rate of normal awareness changes and recursive perception folds in on itself; the fractal nature of reality is beheld.

Trance is how we learn. When we enter a trance state we become 'suggestible', that is we can learn more rapidly from a given input. Clearly this feature of the psyche can be used for good or ill. To heal or harm. People demonstrate reduced critical faculties when we are entranced. Trance is the tool of magick, of marketing, of propaganda and of dreams.

Whatever way they are arrived at (through ritual drama, dance, psychoactives or other methods) these altered states are a core feature of our biology. We can tell that we've always been this way. Today's archaeologists examine the material culture of ancient beliefs through the lens of neurophysiology. Decoding ancient cave paintings and rock art they have discerned the basic elements of the trance process. The shamans' journey of 10,000 years ago and of today arises out of the same neural wiring.

Baphomet for me is this self-conscious process of knowing the techniques and topography of the trance state. That's why there is the antinomian vibe in this figure. It is Lucifer, Promethea, and the Rebel in the Soul. Waking up to a religion in which mystical ecstasy and wonderworking are describable technologies rooted in the body. A religion in which physical sacraments are potent drugs that really do the job. A religion where we realise that we are God. And there is no God but Man.

Shamanism is an adaptation. A series of techniques that have evolved just the same way hands and eyes have evolved. Drumming, innerworld flight, psychoactives, the deployment of these techniques creates trance. In trance we can stimulate immunological responses at both an individual and cultural level. By perceiving the innerworld as spirits we extend our socialising simian style to the experiences that trance gives us access to. This isn't a dumb anthropomorphism but rather a seriously brilliant stratagem. Our brains are built to do complex social relationships. By perceiving thoughts not just as things but rather as entities we can open up channels of communication and control much more readily than if we stick to a farcical 'objective perception'.

This is why I conceptualise Life as the Great Spirit, which I call Baphomet. If you want to talk to something it's polite to address it by name.

So why the horns? Who knows? Perhaps it's the natural tendency of the mind to pay attention to vertical symmetry of faces. The face I see on Baphomet is that of a V shaped form: Nemesis the Warlock, Herne the Hunter. Horns as a deeply embedded icon of power? (Well we've paid attention to horned beats from before even Çatal Hüyük was built.) Horns as the basic duality arising from unity? Perhaps those horns are the fallopian tubes, or the shapes of plants? Or the simple yet profound mathematical fact that one gives rise to two, and then many. A dendritic crown, like neurons or trees.

The Horned deity (which I insist on imagining as both male and female) is a real force emerging in the modern era. Wicca has given rise to the Horned God during the same period that nuclear energy and LSD were discovered. Tiny atoms that rise into whirling mushroom forms (both in the mind and over Japanese cities).

I speak as a shaman. A voice we can all share, a voice that can lead into collective consciousness for the good or ill of our species. The song sings through me, singing all creation into existence. And this act of creation is happening every instant. If the Big Bang happened before time then we might say that it is happening now, will happen. How can the unfolding of the universe be after an event that occurred before time itself?

I pray with tobacco. In front of me the sacred fire of the peyote circle is swept out into the form of a thunderbird. I pray that the sacred medicines can be used wisely and with right attention. I pray that we might soften the hearts of those who would forbid us such things. Great Spirit, whom I call Baphomet, hear my prayer!

Fig 1 – The Peyote Circle.

Satan, Baphomet, Goddess of the World. Our work, the Great Work of Magick, is to wake up. Individually and as a species. Continuous Illumination; this is our Work. But this illumination is the whole process, entering trance and breaking it, and entering a new trance, a new way of being (and again breaking it…). Each time as magicians we move from state to state, trance to trance, we destroy a world. Like the Abraxas chick pecking out into the Mystery. Or as the Ancient Sage of Ankh-Morpork Mrs Cosmopolite would doubtless have observed, "you can't make an omelette without breaking eggs". It is this flow between states that the magician aims to embrace, riding the Shark of Desire through manifestation. The endless parade of what Crowley called the soldier and the hunchback - !?!?!?!?

The magician is the artist of the noosphere. The technician of the sacred. Combining elements into ritual into specific forms of trance to open new possibilities of realisation. To do this work one needs core practice; yoga, meditation, to become skilful in the world. Then one needs to dare, to jump into the Mystery. For me working with Baphomet is like this. There is the silence between beats where we allow the resonance to unfold, time to listen to the universe. This is core practice. Then there are the beats, those rituals that strike trance induced meaning to the world.

A final memory. As I am led into the Chapel (the walls draped in banners of goats' heads, inverted pentagrams and eight rayed stars) I see what is on offer. A test. There is always a test and this time, as the Mass of Chaos B is chanted, I feel the possession take me.

OL - SONUF - VAROSAGAI - GOHU

I - Reign - Over You - Saith

VOUINA - VABZIR - DE - TEHOM - QUADMONAH

The Dragon - Eagle - of - the Primal Chaos

ZIR - ILE - IAIDA - DAYES PRAF - ELILA

I Am - the First - the Highest - That Live In - the First Aether

ZIRDO - KIAFI - CAOSAGO - MOSPELEH - TELOCH

I Am - the Terror - of the Earth - the Horns - of Death

PANPIRA - MALPIRGAY - CAOSAGI

Pouring Down - the Fires of Life - On the Earth

Zazas, Zazas Nasatanada Zazas!

The White Darkness rises up and I am filled with animal intelligence, and rage and power. I am mad, manic, insane, observing my body, my vestigial self-awareness persists (now a pale ghost, tethered to a body filled with some unearthly force). There are voices; an offering is being made to Baphomet. It's shit, fresh and stinking. I'm squatting naked on a pew like a white gargoyle. My hands are long crystalline claws. The faeces do not smell repellent but rather of perfumed rich dark soil. Black Magick. My hands reach out; they grasp the excrement and smear it down my face and body.

Baphomet speaks.

"You in the circle with me, how lovely!"

Years later I find myself in the heart of London. It is August 2009 and for one hour the fourth plinth in Trafalgar Square will be inhabited by Baphomet. I summon the guardians of the four directions; cover the platform with ivy and with roses. The bright, diffused light of the summer's morning turns my body into a black silhouette. The drum calls the spirit, the barbarous names of invocation are vibrated and Baphomet rises up, bringing the wilderness into the heart of the city. Throwing seeds from hir drum, Baphomet rains DNA down onto the earth. And dances and screams.

Fig 2 – Julian Vayne on the fourth plinth in Trafalgar Square, London.

Jerusalem

An operation to revive the Romance of Albion

Soror Res and I visited Tate Britain to see the restaged Blake exhibition that was hung 200 years ago in a room above his brother's hosiery shop in Soho. To accompany the 1809 exhibition of his 'Poetical and Historical Inventions', he published his own catalogue – a 66-page pamphlet that amounts to a manifesto of his artistic beliefs. An admission fee of two shillings and sixpence was charged.

In Tate Britain 10 of the 16 paintings were exhibited. The remainders are lost. This includes what would have been Blake's largest work, some 14x10 ft in size, we still have the catalogue notes about this image;

"In the last battle of King Arthur, only Three Britons escaped; these were the Strongest Man, the Beautifullest Man, and the Ugliest Man ... The Strong Man represents the human sublime. The Beautiful Man represents the human pathetic, which was in the wars of Eden divided into male and female. The Ugly Man represents the human reason. They were originally one man, who was four-fold; he was self-divided, and his real humanity slain on the stems of generation, and the form of the fourth was like the Son of God."

This painting was called 'the Ancient Britons'.

Our aim is to cause the re-discovery of this work (and perhaps the other 5 missing works). More broadly our aim to instigate a new manifestation of the Romantic spirit. This is about, as has been said of Blake "he produced a diverse and symbolically rich corpus, which embraced 'imagination' as 'the body of God', or 'Human existence itself'."

Ritual Process

Statement of Intent: It is our will to manifest the lost art of William Blake.

Begin by looking at the images by Blake that have been printed and posted over the temple walls – declaiming the last verse of the poem 'the Tyger' and repeating this until a signal is given.

Facing the blank canvas which has been placed in the temple try to see and sketch the image of 'the Ancient Britons', as you do so pull the energy of this artwork through that canvass and into the world.

On my signal please stand and sing Jerusalem, imaging this song calling to this image and more generally the romantic spirit back to Albion, this is sung 3 times. First alone, next holding hands, and on the third time with wild dancing.

Banish with laughter.

The Discovery of Witchcraft:

An exploration of the changing face of witchcraft through contemporary interview and personal reflection.

How has the process of discovering witchcraft changed for practitioners over the last twenty years? How does the induction into occultism of the modern teen witch compare to that of teenage witches from previous decades? In this essay I shall be comparing and contrasting the experiences of two witches in order to explore these changes. This comparison of two practitioners, as I will show, can help us to appreciate some of the ways in which witchcraft has developed during the past twenty years.

There are various differences between the experience of pre and post 1990s teen witches that this essay touches upon. One such change is the trend towards solitary Craft practice and away from the more coven based collective forms of Gardnerian/Alexandrian Wicca. Second, that Paganism, in its various guises, is also much more widely understood today and access to information for would-be practitioners is much more easily obtained. The important role of the Internet as a source of information and inspiration for contemporary teen witches is clearly illustrated. Thirdly this essay touches upon the fact that an engagement with Pagan retailers (both physical and latterly via on-line occult supply stores) can be an important part of the process of forging one's identity as a witch. Finally, there are subtle shifts towards a more eclectic form of witchcraft that seem to be emerging as the practices of today's teen witches. This form of the Craft appears to be moving away from the rubric of ritual presented in Gardnerian/Alexandrian Wicca and towards a form of witchcraft, which is more concerned with operational ('results') magick. As well as a change of emphasis, which we might describe as being a move away from religion and towards the magical, there are hints of deeper metaphysical changes. These begin to emerge when our subjects discuss their beliefs about how magick works.

One of the witches I interviewed had become involved with 'the Craft' just over four years ago. The other cast his first magick circle over twenty years previously – me.

My Story

I don't remember a time when I wasn't interested in the occult. Any morsel of information, whether on TV, books or magazines was something that I seized upon with great delight from the earliest age.

By the time I was nine years old I had read my way through everything my local library had to offer in Dewey Decimal 130 - Paranormal phenomena, Occult. The majority of the literature that I read was adult, esoterica with precious little fictional writing. My other significant influence was via TV. Programs such as *The Moon Stallion* (a British television serial made by the BBC in 1978) and *Sapphire and Steel* (a late '70s, early '80s British Sci-Fi series), formed the romantic background to my occult investigations.

Once I reached my teens I had begun my studies in earnest. I had started to meditate regularly, any time that would normally be filled with childish boredom I would sink into a trance and do my best to focus my attention on my breathing.

Meanwhile I was also developing a love of ceremony. My reading had taken me through classics such as the *Key of Solomon* and *The Sacred Magick of Abra-Melin the Mage* and by age thirteen I had encountered writers such as Kenneth Grant and Aleister Crowley. Of all the early literary influences the most significant were the biography of Crowley *The Great Beast* (by the less than complementary John Symonds), and *Diary of a Witch* and *The Complete Art of Witchcraft* by Sybil Leek. Looking back, these books, which I read and re-read, were those that were most evocative of the character of the witch (or magician). As a young man I was looking for heroes, role-models (especially of the hero as apparent anti-hero – a mythic position occupied by Spiderman and Robin Hood as well as figures like Crowley) in addition to learning more about my specialist subject. Meanwhile I was rapaciously working my way through anything and everything I could find for 'technology' – spells, techniques, mystical alphabets, arcane glyphs, ceremonial practices and, in particular, 'folk magick'.

My interest in folk magick arose because of my interest in witchcraft. Although I was familiar with styles of ceremony such as that espoused by the adepts of the Golden Dawn, it was the 'shamanic' approach of spells and practices that (according to most writers at the time) represented the lingering vestiges of pre-Christian belief within European culture that was of greatest appeal. I believed that these Pagan esoteric echoes were most directly present within folklore. In part this interest was supported by the reading material I had available; plenty of books on folk customs and medieval witchcraft (including Margaret Murray's *God of the Witches* and the *Witch Cult in Western Europe*). In another respect this system of magick appealed because of its approachability. My resources at the time didn't stretch to a fully furnished Qabalistic temple and range of suitably coloured robes, however the idea that spells could be as easily performed using a candle and new pin made magick seem more immediate, more achievable with the resources to hand and consequently more exciting. Even so my interest in spellcraft did not overshadow my hunger for ceremonial 'Hermetic' or 'high' ritual. My first 'proper ritual' took place in 1983 (though my first successful spell was some years before). This was a rite to celebrate Halloween and included an attempt to assume the godform of the Egyptian God Set, a far cry from the British folklore spells that I had been so immersed in.

Would I consider my explorations to be part of 'religious' impulse? My own understanding at the time was that religion was about obeying, about accepting one's position in the universal scheme of things, a type of spiritual feudalism. Magick on the other hand represented an autonomous attempt at exploring (and in some measure learning to control) both the inner and outer universes. Although I flirted with the imagery of Satanism I was clear that (as most of my reading suggested) one could not really be a Satanist without accepting the validity of Christianity and since I considered the whole business of monotheism and slavish religion of little interest I did not embrace Satanism even during my most rebellious years (though to the outside observer practices such as invoking Set and, on one occasion burning a Bible just to see if I got anything out of it, might have suggested otherwise).

It was primarily from the 'coffee table' magazine that my mother read - *Titbits* (published for 104 years, it folded in 1984) that I became aware of Wiccans actively working magick in the UK. Janet and Stewart Farrar, authors of a number of significant books on Wicca seemed to be regularly featured in the magazine.

At this stage I was regularly attending events such as the Festival of Mind Body and Spirit in Olympia, London. This large scale 'New Age fayre' was the environment in which I met many people who would later play important roles in my life. It was at such events that I was constantly hoping to find real witches, real magicians and had little or no interest in the New Age or Eastern influenced groups that were present. In 1984 a friend and I had performed the self-initiation ceremony contained in Raymond Buckland's book on Saxon style witchcraft *The Tree*. We had experimented between us with a range of different esoteric techniques, from 'travelling in spirit vision' through to initial forays into the use of psychedelic drugs (primarily mandrake and bay laurel).

By the time I was 15 I had arranged to visit and participate in a coven meeting with a group known as 'Invoking Earth' in Finchley, London. The High Priestess of this Alexandrian lineage coven was Catherine Summers (at the time Catherine Winzar). It was during my second ritual with the 'Invoking Earth' group that I ended up taking the role of High Priest (Lammas 1984). Although friends at school and my parents were very aware of my interest in the occult I was certainly conscious that my interests were 'weird'. I recall very few situations in which my interest in occultism provoked anything other than sidelong glances and vague derision. Fortunately I was not subject to any significant prejudice. Once I left school and began to attend Art College, while still involved with the 'Invoking Earth' group, I became a Goth (sporting the usual Romantic style in dress, taste in music, elaborate hairstyle and so forth). Having become involved with other (generally older) practicing Pagans at a young age I led something of strangely sheltered life in which the majority of my peers were witches and thus found myself as an active participant in an established community and was spared the loneliness and harassment that would have perhaps befallen me had I remained in my home town surrounded by my contemporaries.

Since that time I have found myself teaching occult skills in a variety of situations, have published five books on esoteric topics and lectured and written widely on this subject. Having lived and worked magick in Bristol for some years and later Brighton it was shortly after the birth of my first child that I moved to the quieter rural life of North Devon. Away from major centres of 'alternative culture' I supposed there would be few if any 'teen witches' in evidence, however it has always been important to me to seek out like-minded individuals and so, having been told about a monthly meeting of Pagans and occultists I determined to attend.

Dawn's Story

It was last year at a local Pagan moot (a gathering in a pub) that I met Dawn. Dawn is the joint owner of a gothic clothing and occult supply shop in Barnstaple, Devon. I asked Dawn if she would be prepared to be interviewed so that I could explore the relationship between our experiences of becoming involved with witchcraft. My aim was to get a picture both of Dawn's entry into the Craft, and to investigate how she conceptualised her occultism. As a young woman with a fairly prominent role in the local occult scene (particularly as the owner of a shop that is a Mecca for young Goths in the area) she seemed an ideal choice.

I began by asking Dawn how she would describe herself. "A witch"[1] was her immediate response, which she defined as "…to do with practicing magick and observing certain codes, for example the Wiccan Rede, and being into practices such as herbs, crystals and healing."

I asked "So how did you get involved in this area?"

Dawn explained that she started her journey when she was about 15, going through her "Goth phase" being inspired by films such as *The Crow*, the graphic novels of Neil Gaiman and the writing of Wiccan author Vivianne Crowley. She also explained that for her, and more particularly for the friends she was exploring this material with, it was, "…for show, a fashion thing". But that it did seem to resonate with a particular sense of being. "I've always felt that I was different. [I was] fascinated by nature, the sea used to fascinate me and I'd go for walking at night and traipse across the fields to see the stars."

It was this "affinity with nature" that spurred Dawn on to explore the occult and Pagan material available via the on-line store Amazon during her first pregnancy (at age 21).

"I bought some books, Scott Cunningham and *The Wicca Handbook* (by Eileen Holland), I thought, maybe it's time for me to get into this properly. And then I started the shop ['spikeys' of Barnstaple] and now I shop on a daily basis for witchcraft and Pagan goods."

Although some might claim that witchcraft today is over commercialised for the 'Buffy generation', for both Dawn and I it was the commercial world that formed an essential point of contact. Dawn has gone on to run a successful esoteric business but I also became a retailer of occult goods fairly early on. I founded a mail order incense business ('sator Square') and made and sold incenses at the Camden Psychic Forum, London. Perhaps in witchcraft there is something in the tradition that inspires its adherents to provide services (magickal paraphernalia, incenses, oils, divinatory readings etc). Perhaps this is a resonance with the social position of the witch (or cunning man/woman) as provider of magickal skills to his or her community. (The role the cunning folk primarily before the 20th century is explored by Owen Davies in his book *Cunning-folk: Popular Magick in English History*.)

For me, meeting other people was an essential feature of getting involved with witchcraft. Much more than doing my own practices or rituals the sense of community and of being involved was crucial. As someone who has worked magick in covens, edited journals and written and broadcasted, I wondered if this desire for community with others was something Dawn shared.

But for Dawn, though her work brings her into contact with large numbers of people interested in the occult, her story has been much more solitary.

"Other than a few Pagan moots I've been to I've done everything on my own. It's all been through reading lots and lots of different stuff and not necessarily 'magical' books. When I was 15 there were the 5 of us and we did little things like go and find a circle of trees in the woods [and try out casting a circle] but I don't think we took it as seriously as we could have.

I've been working to teach myself all these bits and pieces and having the responsibility of the shop means I don't want to give people bad advice. We do get kids coming in saying stuff like 'black magick is so cool' and I'll speak to them and change their conceptions and they'll go away thinking 'oh alright then I won't go and try that…'."

Some of the difference here may well be determined by changes in the structure of witchcraft over time. For me the coven was the unit in which witchcraft was worked and so there was an immediate assumption, on my part, that I needed to find a small working group to practice with and learn from. There was also more emphasis on the idea of Wicca as an initiatory tradition, the view of the Craft as a 'mystery religion' (that Vivianne Crowley presents in *Wicca: The Old Religion in the New Age*). Although I know from friends who run reasonably public covens today that, post-Buffy, they are inundated with enquiries from prospective initiates[2] the model of the solitary witch is much more firmly established. Rae Beth's book *Hedge Witch* (1992) and the work of Marian Green *A Witch Alone* and subsequent works clearly developed the notion of the solitary witch. The upsurge of interest in 'traditional witchcraft' and the model of the witch as the cunning man/woman and of course, the predominantly solo (or at least not 'cultish') presentation of witchcraft in Buffy, have also been important factors. It is perhaps less essential to join anything to do witchcraft these days. The existence of exemplars of solitary witchcraft and the abundance of user-friendly information, through both print and the Internet, have supported the move away from witchcraft and the Wiccan cult being synonymous.

While aware of bodies such as the Pagan Federation Dawn said that she wasn't affiliated with any organisations. However her business has a presence in cyberspace, which is linked to www.witchvox.com (www.spikeys.co.uk)

I asked Dawn to explain a little more about the sources of information that had influenced her:

"Scott Cunningham is a big influence because he puts thing so simply. Eileen Holland's *The Wiccan Handbook*. I've got a few spell books for Christmas from well-meaning friends but I tend to find them rather over complicated and prefer to write my own spells. I'm currently studying a course in magical herbalism and a crystal healing certificate. Oh yes and Neil Gaiman of course."

Was the Internet a valuable source of information when Dawn was first engaging with the Craft?

"[There are] Lots of groups out there on Yahoo, MSN, Children of Artemis and Wicca.com, spellsandmagic.com – lots of sites you need to take with a pinch of salt, you've got sites out there dedicated to destructive magick. Now I tend to rely on books as I'm in the fortunate position of having all these suppliers [for the shop] and they've got fantastic libraries!"

This seems to be a general trend at the moment with other newer witches I've spoken to. Printed books still seem to be the key resource. The Internet provides a 'transport layer' to information (searching for texts, exchanging ideas with others and getting vignettes of data) but for serious study the contemporary British witch is perhaps more likely to consult a physical text (although it is highly likely that the book will have been discovered and perhaps ordered over the net).

For Dawn printed journals were not an important personal influence. Although aware of the Pagan Federation magazine *Pagan Dawn* she hadn't read it. This is a significantly different situation to the one in which I entered the Craft. The rise of desktop publishing (in the 1980s) produced a proliferation of esoteric journals, functioning at both local and national level. Although a small number of printed esoteric magazines continue to be published in the UK the Internet has taken up many of the services these journals originally served.

Other influences that Dawn identified were *Harry Potter*, *The Craft*, *Charmed* and, of course, *Buffy the Vampire Slayer*.

Dawn explained how new witches have, in her view, the sense that the information they need is easily accessible:

"Because of the Internet they can go out and immediately find out about it [ie magick] – I came across a site that had a list of all the spells ever used in Buffy and translations of all the Latin! Out of all the TV shows I'd say that Buffy is the most responsible, you do see the downfall of Willow because of her misuse of magick."

Fortunately when I first became involved in witchcraft the Satanic ritual abuse (SRA) panic had yet to emerge in the UK[3]. Although Dawn was aware that SRA was a recent feature in the history of British Paganism she was unconcerned about possible negative social implications of being known as a witch.

"I don't exactly disguise the fact that I practice – I mean I wear a hoody that says 'protected by witchcraft' on it. I don't hide what I believe but I don't push it on people either.

People say 'why do you believe in magick' and I can give them an example of when a spell has worked stunningly well."

Indeed Dawn's outlook on the future of British and perhaps global culture, and the role of witchcraft within that was very optimistic. She gave the example of how a few years ago it would have been unthinkable that a transsexual person could have won a game show such as Big Brother[4]. In her view this was a sign of an increasingly open and tolerant society.

Was this increase in openness a feature of the 'New Age'?

"There is definitely an upsurge in it [witchcraft]. I have big feeling that something major is going to happen – the Age of Aquarius is apparent because people are turning their back on organised religion and because of the Internet and freedom of information. If someone says 'did you see so-and-so?' I can just Google it and immediately I can get that information. Aquarius is a scientific age and the Internet encompasses that…It's now acceptable for coloured, gay, transsexual people to be in society and everybody is looking for ways to be more fulfilled in themselves and if they can do that through a personal relationship with deity then that's what they will do. It is all about personal identity; [witchcraft is] empowering and proactive. And it's not just about you; if you study herbs [for example] from a magickal perspective you'll start to see the healing possibilities of these things and how you can help other people."

Understanding magick

So what is the relationship between magick and religion? This is a question that has concerned a number of academics, most famously James Frazer, and more recently Ronald Hutton. The relationship between these two concepts was one I was keen to have Dawn's thoughts on since it often serves to make explicit, underlying structures of belief. Asking 'how does magick work?' of a witch provides an opportunity for the respondent to provide an ontological exegesis.

My own association with the Craft also involves a process of exploring these two realms. From my earliest interest in Wicca I was aware that this was a religion (indeed *The* Old Religion) yet the notion of religion for me remained linked, as described above, to monotheism and a servile approach to the universe. Magick seemed to represent something different to that, a fundamentally different approach to interacting with 'the sacred' (though I was equally unhappy with what I considered to be the naive idea that magicians should aim to be 'all powerful'). I don't think that my own unease about identifying myself as a 'religious Pagan' or Wiccan is that unusual. I suspect that this unwillingness to identify with a religion is one of the factors that has led to a movement by younger witches away from the religion of Wicca and towards forms of the Craft that seem to be less concerned with elements such as priesthood, initiatory and apostolic succession. I think this suggestion is borne out by the distinctions that Dawn makes between magick and religion, below.

Dawn explains, "…most people will agree that there is one creator but wouldn't necessarily be sure about putting names or worshipping deities, because witchcraft is founded on the principle rule of 'an it harm none, do what you will', it doesn't mean that you have to include deity names, and I think that if people feel you have to do that it's going to put them off so I try to get across that no you don't have to do that if you're not comfortable with it because as long as they're not hurting anyone with what they are doing, performing the spells, then that's not going to turn out badly for them. So you've got Wicca which is one religion of witchcraft and witchcraft [which is] the act of practicing magick."

So can anyone do a witchcraft spell even if they are from a different religion? Does the magical process of witchcraft irrespective of one's religious beliefs?

Dawn explains, "Witchcraft is actually a science as opposed to something mystical. You read all the books and they always say about 'vibrations'. The way I perceive magick is that when people pray to God or whatever they are verbally connecting with the planet and that's a form of vibration (like the vibrating air) and magick just takes ingredients that, from my point of view, have been scientifically proven through experiments over the years…you've got peppermint which is good for money and aventurine which is also good for that, and by taking items with a different but similar vibration [and putting them together] you create a stronger signal to send out to the universe."

Dawn supported her argument by drawing on some material on quantum physics she had been reading. This was what might be called a 'literal scientific' model of magick rather than 'metaphorical psychological' (see below). However there is also a strong relativistic, perspectival aspect to Dawn's conception of magick. When discussing how the Gods exist she elaborated using an analogy drawn from Neil Gaiman's *Sandman*.

"In *Sandman*, the bit where Morpheus [the central character and avatar of dreams] dies and they all say 'how come dreams still exist'? It's explained by saying about the diamond and each facet is just somebody else's point of view. Well that made sense to me for the deity argument. So the diamond is the creator and all the facets are the different deities, each a different point of view."

The discovery of the reality of magick brings with it a certain amount of soul searching about what one could or should do with this power, especially with a power which might either be unlimited or at least in many senses 'undetectable'[5]. Like Plato's Gyges with his ring of invisibility, the question we must ask is: who can be trusted to wield such power without becoming corrupt? (Plato answers: "Philosophers." Tolkien answers: "Nobody.")

For Dawn it is the Wiccan Rede that it provides the acid test.

"As long as you apply the Wiccan Rede to everything you do you can't go wrong – what annoys me these days is that there are lots of spell books, or in teenage magazines that get hold of the idea of Wicca and turn it into something else. So many books that say 'how to get a man to love you' and as far as I'm concerned that's black magick because it's doing something that is against somebody else's will and without their permission. So I think so long as the spell doesn't force anybody to do anything that is against their will or without their permission, as long as it isn't going to hurt anyone else I don't think there is a problem with that. A simple love spell might seem innocent enough but that is a form of black magick and can only end badly for you – I mean take what happened to Xander in Buffy."[6]

Where I might have illustrated a similar position by appeal to one of the tales told by Dion Fortune or Stewart Farrar, Dawn selects her example from the mythology of Buffy.

Although I prefer to avoid terms such as 'black magick' my own beliefs do accord with Dawn's in many ways. If we take the term 'will' within the Wiccan Rede to equate with Crowley's use of the term (as the 'true Will' which is akin to the *te* of Taoism, one's 'Inner Nature') I would agree that performing magick that attempts to thwart the Will of another person (or indeed oneself) is likely to 'end badly'.

So, in order to access the power of magick, what are the key areas of knowledge that a witch should seek?

Dawn explains:

"The main ingredients with which you write a spell are candles, herbs and crystals and the witchcraft tools. Although with herbs and crystals you can take a specialist route with healing, aromatherapy etc., I think that everybody should have a general idea of what a good load of herbs [to have] would be. Scott Cunningham in his books said that every witch should have a certain collection of herbs because they can be applied to so many spells, so that, mint for example, most people in the magickal community will know that's good for money spells and prosperity and that if you're a beginner witch and that's all you know about the herb then that's fine because that will still help you focus on your goal. You don't need to know the scientific name or how the essential oil is made or what it's a good incense for. So my advice to people, when they come to the shop, is get a general knowledge of herbs and crystals, the tools of the trade and probably moon phases because of when to cast the spell."

I certainly made a detailed study of correspondences myself when I started out in witchcraft. Delving into books such as Crowley's 777 and pouring through more modern texts to garner an understanding of the sympathetic relationship between colours, gems, planets, herbs and so forth. For Dawn understanding these relationships is vital when it comes to 'writing' spells.

I noticed in this interview an interesting turn of phrase, used twice, rather than 'casting' spells Dawn talks about 'writing' them. Perhaps this derives from the idea that the process of spellcraft requires it to be first written in a grimoire (literally 'spelled out') - the magickal act is built first as a literary object before it becomes a performative rite. On reflection after this interview Dawn elaborates (by email):

"When I refer to 'writing' spells as opposed to casting, it is because for me taking the time to create something myself rather than take a spell from a book helps me a) focus and b) research further where necessary. Once I have them written the spell it has become a personal work which has more meaning for me and enables me to concentrate and raise personal power more effectively."

My own explorations of spellcraft rapidly led me to the belief that it wasn't so much the inherent vibrations of things (candles, crystals, resins etc) but their capacity to focus the mind in a particular direction that was of importance. Perhaps this view, undoubtedly influenced in my case by 1970s parapsychology and the relativistic trends in occultism that emerged in the 1980s as 'chaos magick', represents a retreat from a 'scientific' material basis for magick and an attempt to ground magick more directly in the language of psychology, parapsychology and psychoanalysis (especially of the Jungian school). My approach (which might be seen as reaching its apotheosis in what has become known within chaos magick as 'empty handed magick' – i.e. magick performed with little or no ritual paraphernalia and minimal physical activity) holds that there is no inherent power of mint to bring about riches but it is the psychological connection forged in the mind of the spell caster that does the job. Magick for me then is perhaps more 'all in the mind' than it is for Dawn, although we should be wary of extending this metaphor too far. For both of us, the occult axiom of 'as above, so below' claims that the Cartesian apparent separation of mind and body (or the material verses mental words) is illusionary.

Dawn's comment 'most people in the magickal community will know that [mint is] good for money spells' set me thinking. Mint is not an herb I would immediately have picked for such a charm. Although Dawn and I clearly shared some of the same points of reference it seemed to me that there might be significant differences we were glossing over because we assumed we shared a mutual language and common underlying structures of belief. So, just to check that I understood what Dawn was talking about with her use of the term 'witchcraft tools' I asked her to list them.

"Pentacle, athame, wand, censer, boline and candles, the things you would place on an altar."

Interestingly she does not list the cup as a key tool, perhaps simply an oversight on her part but also perhaps an omission indicative of the changing face of witchcraft. In Wicca the cup is a crucial item. As a Goddess focused cult the cup is of core importance symbolically. As container for consecrated wine it is also an essential tool for ceremonies such as the Great Rite and provides the sacramental end to most Wiccan rites. The cup is predominantly social. Wine is the sacred drug of the Wiccan cult and sharing wine is the symbolic equivalent of the Catholic Mass; the literal collective absorption of divine power. 'Cakes and Wine' is an important motif of Wiccan rite that reflects and engenders social cohesion within the coven (i.e. ends the rite and begins the party). Having done solitary Wiccan style ceremonies myself (drawing on the rites penned by Doreen Valiente) where the cup is still a feature, it always felt a little odd raising a glass to the Gods, taking a sip myself but having no-one else to pass the cup to. Perhaps for the more solitary style of Craft that Dawn pursues the role of the cup is reduced for this reason.

Dawn mentions the boline, the white handled knife that is used for "…cutting herbs, harvesting plants and doing other magickal chores for which they [witches] don't use the athame." The boline, derived from the Key of Solomon is well established as a Wiccan tool and remains common to Dawn's brand of Craft. However the cords (mentioned as one of the tools in the Witches Rune power raising chant) are absent from Dawn's list. This makes perfect sense as the use of cords is most appropriate in group ritual (as binding for initiatory or trance work, or for spell casting by pulling and knotting). The scourge, that most contested of Gardnerian Wiccan pieces of paraphernalia, is also absent.

On the subject of occult paraphernalia, should one makes one's own tools or is buying them okay? Dawn's opinion on this chimes in with my own.

"Because witchcraft is a very personal thing you can't generalise – so if you like working in wood you'll probably want to make your own wand but if you don't have the talent in making things you shouldn't feel bad about buying them."

Reflections

I certainly found it revealing to speak with Dawn about her experiences. While there were many similarities in our initial phase of engagement with witchcraft there were also differences both in the content that I can relay in this text and also in the tenor of our experiences.

Let us consider the question posed at the beginning of this essay; namely in what ways is the discovery of witchcraft different today for modern teen witches from my experience of twenty plus years ago?

For me witchcraft was much more literally occult; a secret, a rare thing. Gathering information about the Craft, though by no means impossible, was far from as straightforward as 'Googling' the Internet. The technology of the Internet, coupled with cultural notions of freedom of information have had a powerful effect. The creating of popular cultural icons of magick (particularly through the TV series *Buffy the Vampire Slayer*) means that those interested in witchcraft can now 'plug in' quite directly to the knowledge they desire.

Perhaps the most marked difference is the move from witchcraft being synonymous with Wicca. Witchcraft for Dawn and her peers seems to be predominantly a technology where, although belief is important, it is the 'vibrations' of the components of a spell that are the keys to its efficacy. In this respect contemporary witchcraft has come to occupy a position closer to practices associated with occult traditions such as Macumba, Santeria or Voudou. The magick is 'low tech' in a ritual sense (usually consisting of short chants or poems rather than the more Hermetic style soliloquies of ritual magick or Alexandrian/Gardnerian Wicca), grounded in the use of actual power objects rather than a more psychological approach and able to be carried out effectively whatever the religious belief system of the practitioner (in much the same way that a Brazilian Catholic can quite effectively and without any ontological difficulty use an Umbanda spell).

Of course this does not deny the importance of the 'psychological' or inner processes of successful spellcraft (what Peter Carroll calls 'sleight of mind'). Dawn's email to me after my interview explains:

"I referred to the vibrations of herbs, crystals etc, it is my view that these alone will not carry a spell. It's like a car battery (vibrations), it's powerful in its own right but you won't get anywhere without the car (personal power and focus)."

It will be interesting to observe those witches who have joined the Craft as part of the 'Buffy generation' will develop. Will they tend to remain as solo practitioners or will the need to establish themselves as a defined cultural group create the emergence of new forms of collaborative magickal working? The continuing success of large scale events such as Witchfest (organised by the Children of Artemis)[7] , conferences arranged by the Pagan Federation[8] and others, would seem to suggest that our new breed of witches are not content with exclusively on-line communities. Shall we see new coven group structures emerging and if so how will they be constructed? How will the Internet play a part in determining how these groups are formed and how alliances are forged and broken? And perhaps most interesting of all, with the tendency towards openness and freedom of information that Dawn identifies, as well as the need for proactive self-discovery, will the witch begin to be sought out by non-witches as a magickal specialist, ushering in the return of the role of the cunning man and woman in broader culture?

What we can see is that the Craft, or more generally what we might call (after Kenneth Grant) the 'magical revival', is successfully continuing in our culture. That in the brief period that marks the difference in time between my first steps of the path of magick and those of Dawn magick has changed. It has adapted to new technological developments and the emergence of new pop-culture icons. That it will continue to do so successfully for the foreseeable future seems highly likely.

Watching the apocalypse

A friend of mine works as a psychologist specialising in 'organisational development', basically what humans get up to when in groups. He describes his work, with typical brilliant simplicity, as 'exploring what it is that we find ourselves doing'. So, with that approach in mind, what is it what we find ourselves doing as we approach another date packed by culture with a payload of apocalyptic pronouncements?

A while ago I found myself watching a film called *2012*. The movie (for those who haven't seen it) is rather like watching a filmic version of one of those awesome John Martin paintings. Huge fissures open in the earth, lightning punctures the clouds, the seas boil, stones fall from the heavens – you get the picture. Although there is a something approximating a narrative the movie is really all about watching a CGI-tastic version of *Koyaanisqatsi*. The world is turned upside-down, LA is sucked into the San-Andrea fault, a tsunami floods across the Himalayas.

So what do we find ourselves doing as 2012 approaches? We are watching the cataclysm, over and over again, in the news, in films, in literature. Endlessly rehearsing The End. Our are eyes (for most of us mediated through the TV camera) raised to heaven as glass and suited bodies rain down from the world trade centre. We look up, disrupted from the everyday reality of our lives, transfixed by the violence and ungraspable scale of what we are witnessing. We know well before the headlines of the next day that we are witnessing at least the beginning of the apocalypse.

A more recent catastrophe. The BP Deep Water Horizon leak. This time our gaze is directed downward, across the vast sheets of oil sliding through the blue waters of the Gulf of Mexico. Over a kilometre beneath the ocean the ooze that feeds our machines spews out. There is a bloom of death in the sea. On the once white sands the mute figures of seabirds, limp with that same dead eyed stare typical of the inmates of refugee or prison camps.

And thanks to the wonder of information technology; film, TV and the

Internet, all our eyes are witness to these tragedies, again and again, reloading the content, buffering the video. We can watch these events many times over, indulge ourselves, and fetishize those disasters. The plane plunging into the towers, again and again. The shouts from the hundreds of children inside Beslan school Number One. Computers allow us to place these events in our own narrative, harnessing their power to promote our own agenda. The truth about 9/11, 7/7, the propaganda mash-up is viral.

Many of these events are awesome in their scale, filmic in their grandeur. They are like mountains where we might expect to find a sublime rapture but instead experience a vast horror. Scale is a major part of this and the 2012 complex of ideas is all about scale. There is no escaping that date. Unless we elect to depart the wheel of Samsara by suicide it cannot be avoided. It is an inexorable certainty, which will sweep the world whether we like it, or not. It's much bigger than any of us. Unstoppable. Our puny bodies or individual selves, our choices (which Western culture is so fixated on,) will mean absolutely nothing in the face of this inevitable something.

A volcano spews ash into the air. The prospect of planes falling from the sky has replaced the divine lightning strikes of vengeful deities. And in today's hyper-connected, hyper-real world we know there is simply nowhere to run.

The revolution may not be televised but the apocalypse probably will be. Probably in glorious high definition 3D with special glasses designed to reduce the glare as we accidentally create a supernova in the large hadron collider.

Of course this desire to witness or imagine the end of times isn't new. Ever since the first Zoroastrian mused over the eschatological possibilities contained in The Avestra. That holy book details how, at the end of the 'third time', there will be a battle between the forces of good and those of evil. Good will triumph and the dead will then experience an embodied resurrection. After this the forces of good will arrange a last judgement. The Gods will melt the mountains so that a river of metal flows across the land. Both currently living and resurrected dead must walk through the fiery river. The righteous will experience it as a river of warm milk but the wicked will be burnt and be driven down to hell where the molten metal will destroy any lingering impurity in the world.

This basic format is being played out now in the suggestion that 2012 will mark some sort of great discontinuity. Whether history ends, the biosphere collapse and/or we become transmogrified into beings of pure energy, the storyline is much the same. A great event, way outside of human control, will re-form the world. Sifting the wheat from the chaff as part of the process, and ushering in a new age.

The esoteric tradition in the west also is infused with this story. Here it is presented as the movement of aeons; periods of psycho-historic time that mark the transition between different mystical dispensations. As inevitable and unavoidable as the sweep of the sun across the surface of the earth.

For the arch-magus Aleister Crowley the 20th century marked the Equinox of the Gods. Horus, the child of Osiris and Isis, was in the ascendancy.

Crowley writes in *The Book of Thoth*:
"He [Horus] rules the present period of 2,000 years, beginning in 1904. Everywhere his government is taking root. Observe for yourselves the decay of the sense of sin, the growth of innocence and irresponsibility, the strange modifications of the reproductive instinct with a tendency to become bi-sexual or epicene, the childlike confidence in progress combined with nightmare fear of catastrophe, against which we are yet half unwilling to take precautions.

Consider the outcrop of dictatorships, only possible when moral growth is in its earliest stages, and the prevalence of infantile cults like Communism, Fascism, Pacifism, Health Crazes, Occultism in nearly all its forms, religions sentimentalized to the point of practical extinction.

Consider the popularity of the cinema, the wireless, the football pools and guessing competitions, all devices for soothing fractious infants, no seed of purpose in them.

Consider sport, the babyish enthusiasms and rages, which it excites, whole nations disturbed by disputes between boys.

Consider war, the atrocities which occur daily and leave us unmoved and hardly worried. We are children."

We are children indeed. Dwarfed by the awesome scale of the events that loom over us. More than Crowley's 'half unwilling to take precautions' everyday we live beneath a sky which holds more and more of heat. The weather patterns are breaking down, the ice sheets melting. Yet still we type on our computers, drive to work, eat our food that relies for its production on oil, invisibly pushing carbon dioxide into the sky.

However Crowley, again in *The Book of Thoth*, remains optimistic.

"It is a thought far from comforting to the present generation that 500 years of dark ages are likely to be upon us...fortunately today we have brighter torches and more torch-bearers".

Of course like the Zoroastrians we get around the personal horror of the apocalypse by imagining that we (ourselves, our family, our tribe or perhaps at least all the Good People) will somehow be saved. There is the mass of people; those nameless, innumerable figures crowding into feeding centres and shanty towns, they are the cannon fodder for the end times. But perhaps some of us, those of us who have planted our own vegetables, or bought a gun, or simply lived honourable and spiritual lives – we shall be saved.

Thing is these days no one's quite certain how to ensure that you end up in the chosen few. Of course for those people with a comforting literalist religion things are just as simple as they were a thousand years ago; all the Catholics, faggots, blacks and liberals will burn in hell fire leaving the world free to be re-populated by God-fearing upstanding folks. However even in such sealed worlds it's painfully obvious that there are several mutually exclusive groups who claim that is they who shall inherit the earth. So best err on the side of caution. The Lord is bound to best protect those who protect themselves. Faith in providence is naturally tempered by a healthy dose of survivalist acumen.

Neopagans, who perhaps suggest that 2012 could be about a 'shift in human consciousness' where we might re-integrate our species with the Gaian supermind, are also coming to the same conclusions. The current vogue for forest schooling, Ray Mears style bush craft, lighting fires with sticks and making your own fishing spears, has a shadow side. We learn to make fire from first principles in part because we are afraid. Afraid that one day all the matches will run out. Those in the aftermath of some great upheaval we will need to flee to the woods. They know the difference between dogs' mercury and ground elder might mean the difference between life and death.

Of course running away into the wilderness, especially in the landscape of countries such as England is easier said than done. YouTube, the automatic number plate recognition system, Google earth, GPS, infrared helicopter cameras – it all adds up to a multi-layered panopticon. We fear, especially those of us who live in countries with high tech post-industrial cultures, that wherever we run, *they* will know.

Some people like to place the locus for the coming 2012 apocalypse in a natural event. The flipping of the magnetic poles, an alignment between our solar system and some mysterious force lurking in the core of our galaxy. But it's not only the naturally occurring calamity that scares it. It's what the people, and especially the government, would do in such a situation. Internment camps, draconian edicts, martial law. We imagine that as the meteor hurtling towards earth becomes visible to the naked eye the impact would be (pardon the pun) the last of our problems. Unhinged, people would go mad. Revert to some terrible every-man-for-himself violence. David Bowie sings of what the knowledge that we've got just five years left does to us;

"A girl my age went off her head, hit some tiny children If the black hadn't a-pulled her off, I think she would have killed them."

Rather than a vision of facing the threat of natural disaster shoulder to shoulder we fear that viciousness will emerge. Violent anarchy and the rule of the gun would result. Such a fear infects most end time scenarios. Perhaps this sense is because true violence, true tragedy is a human artifice. More than that, since World War I, we have come to see how we humans can destroy our own species on an industrial scale. Machine guns, gas, the final solution, the atom bomb. The 'banality of evil' that political theorist Hannah Arendt described in the Third Reich has etched terrible echoes in our souls. In *The Green Fields of France* by Eric Bogle he addresses his song to a fallen soldier from WWI.

> "And I can't help but wonder now Willie MacBride
> do all those who lie here know why they died?
> Did you really believe them when they told you the cause?
> Did you really believe them that this war would end wars?
> Well the suffering, the sorrow, the glory, the shame -
> the killing and dying - it was all done in vain.
> Oh Willie MacBride, it's all happened again
> and again, and again, and again, and again."

It's this industrial, unforgiving repetition, the eternal return of human cruelty that runs beneath the surface of even the most love and light visions of 2012. Why? Because we modern people know it happens; the killing fields of Cambodia, the Bosnian genocide, the Rwanda horror – *'and again, and again, and again, and again.'*

Then there are those scenarios where the end comes not in a bang but with a quiet whimper. In the P.D.James' novel *Children of Men* the world is in chaos because human fertility has dropped to zero. The gnawing madness of this situation is suggested as the reason that the world is in such turmoil. After all, without children what's the point? In a dystopian Britain large numbers of people take part in government sanctioned mass drownings, the 'Quietus' ceremony. In the film adaptation of the novel Quietus becomes a suicide kit, advertised on billboards and bearing the slogan 'you decide when'.

Children of Men is an exploration of the social effects of demographic changes. Our planet currently supports over 6.6 billion humans and although we've done a remarkably good job in ensuring that only a select few have access to medicine, decent food or clean water, we're still breeding like, well, rats. Whatever End Time we imagine the main trouble is always the mass of humanity. For some of us this is the fear of vigilant groups and berserk military. For the Boyd Rice's of this world it's about being drowned in the breeding avalanche of inane human flesh.

"Do you ever think about

what a lovely place the world would be

Without all the people

That make life so unpleasant?"

And rather than the rise of a totalitarian state being something to be feared, perhaps it's about time we really got to grips with the Malthusian population crisis. Boyd Rice again;

"I say, bring back the Circus Maximus

For starters

Unless these weeds are dealt with

They'll poison everything

They are poisoning everything

We need a gardener

A brutal gardener

A thorough, thoughtful gardener

An iron gardener

Whatever happened to Vlad the Impaler?

Where's Genghis Kahn when you need him?

Or Roi d'Ys?

Ayatollah Khomeini?

Adolf Hitler?

Benito Mussolini?

Nero?

Diocletian?

Kitchener?

Come back! Come back!"

The last big apocalyptic date 2000AD passed without much incident. For that date there was the predicted millennium meltdown of Y2K (which was only averted by some magickal work I and three colleagues did). We were told that this hidden trip switch was, quite probably, going to crash all the computers in the world. This was supposed to set in motion a chain of events that would lead to the accidental deployment of military systems, the breakdown of nuclear reactors and the possibility that you might not be able to use your debit card to buy beers on the run up towards midnight. With 2012 there is no obvious earthly connection to any terrestrial event. This has freed us up somewhat to start creating visions of this End Time that have a more cosmic bent.

Terence McKenna, using a combination of brain melting drugs, FORTRAN running on an old CDC 6400 computer and the I Ching, famously plumped for 2012 as the historical moment of 'maximum novelty'. His theory, although suitably packaged as something emerging from the techosphere of computing, is no different to that of Crowley. His interpretations of history are more interesting in what they tell us about the mythos of modern humans than any supposed objective reality of the model.

The 'glittering object at the end of time' (which could of course have been Terry's perception of the tumour growing in his brain) is a moment when, in some interpretations, everything happens simultaneously. This is very similar to my own views on the nature of death (see *Now That's What I Call Chaos Magick* and *Magick Works*). We enter a space where all memories are recalled at once. There is no 'after' the event in the case of physical death because the brain ceases to function. In cultural terms if the December Solstice of 2012 were such a moment then it would indeed be a 'death'.

The question arises about what comes next (in as far as it is meaningful to talk about a 'next' in this situation). A translation into some kind of non-material body is usually favoured at this point. McKenna was delightfully obscure (or playful) about what he thought would happen next. Perhaps we would become beings of information, without physical bodies. Maybe human history would end in its isolated form because we'd have first contact with true aliens – who knows?

The resurrection in some altered form takes us right back to that Zoroastrian story. Indeed resurrection is the mythic DNA that keeps much of our mythscape running. Central to all forms of monotheism (even to Buddhism in the form of the enlightenment discontinuity) the dying and resurrected God (or self) brings us back again to the core of the 2012 myth.

So what do we find ourselves doing? We are obsessively watching the signs, waiting for an event so huge that we can do nothing about it. We are fearful that as this event takes place society will break down. We fear we cannot escape but must put our faith in those things (beliefs, resources, rituals) that will help us through the crisis. Once the catastrophe is done with we shall rise again. The earth will be cleansed of all dross and we shall live forever in peace. Sound familiar?

2012 is nothing more than an echo of our own terror. It is modelled on the basic eschatological storyline roughed out in the Middle East many thousands of years ago. It is how we deal with the certainty of our own death. How we fantasise about surviving our End and rising again. The fact that we see this as a literal historic process tells us simply that we have failed to escape from the monotheist trap of linear time. Rather than appreciate the fact that whatever happens we live, die, are reabsorbed and live again. Failure to create myths that speak of this cycle leaves us with no alternative than to make sense of the world through these eschatological stories, to sit in the isolated darkness fretting over our own death.

If we need an eschatology, if we really can't get along without filling this mythological niche in our psychic ecology how about this one? An End Times prediction I'm happy to stake my reputation on;

In about 5,000,000,000 years' time the sun will go out.

The Rite to Roam

All Over This Wasteland

In the bushes. Nothing special, just the kind of municipal planting one finds in new towns and suburban developments. A rectangular area thick with one type of deciduous shrub (I have no ideas of the species). The space would later be colonised by garages, mostly built by my father. The leaves of those bushes were vivid green in spring, later turning an almost bluish tone and lastly fading into curled crisps of russet.

It was here that I built my first temple.

Adults sometimes assume that what we might call religious or spiritual concerns are of no interest to children. For me at least this wasn't the case. I was perhaps seven, maybe younger, when I discovered 'the Orb'. The Orb was an emerald-green-faceted bead of glass, no larger than a pea. I decided that it was special, very special, in fact that it was a God. I scrambled my way into the heart of the bushes, the darkness of this miniature forest. There, among the scraps of litter and cracked clay, I created a pyramid. This stepped ziggurat was the podium upon which my small God sat. The Orb was installed and I began a daily ritual of worship. Picking my way through the low canopy of leaves, my nose close to the dusty earth, to the shrine I had made. Here I would make offerings of perfume (Swizzels Parma Violets), flowers and my own hair. Sometimes sorcery comes quite naturally to the young.

I never forgot The Orb (though its whereabouts now I can hardly guess). But what stayed with me was that secret sense that comes from being in the woods, especially in the woods doing magick.

Being outside, surrounded by natural forms (whether it be trees in a plantation or ancient wildwood) can induce in me a rapture of delight. Sometimes this comes from a small space. Like the bushes by my family home, the fairy hollow in a tree, the tiny crook of a stream, these can invoke this most powerful of feelings. I am at once me and more than me. I am a creature moving across the land. I am connected by my sight, my breath, my motion to this much larger cosmos. Tiny spaces can do this as easily as the awesome void of the desert or the looming forms of great mountains.

I was captivated as a child by all those diminutive worlds that one encounters. Rock pools, tiny cone shaped fungus, the cracks in pavements from which emerged robotic ants. Growing up where I did there was always plenty of wasteland. Places that had, and would again, be filled with concrete and brick and human structures. Always in an indeterminate state between having been built on, and awaiting new developments. Like an uneasy cat in Schrödinger's box, wasteland hovers between the worlds. Here punks and naughty boys gather to drink, sniff glue and undertake essential experimental work (for example, what happens when you chuck an aerosol can on a fire?). Here was broken glass and wood and all kinds of half-remembered detritus. So far from the sea as I was, this was the place I could plunder for urban flotsam and jetsam. A crooked metal rod would be my Martian wand. Foundation slabs of concrete would be the stage upon which I conducted my childish rituals, drawing sigils, circles and mystical signs.

The most impressive thing about the wasteland, as those of us who love it will know, is that it is far from desolate. Bindweed drowns the hulks of burnt out cars, teasels strike up between rubble hillocks. Brambles finger their way across the splitting tarmac. Birds and scurrying animals abound. These are the pioneer species, so full of thrusting, lusting life. In the brief gap we humans leave, wild nature comes rushing in and inundates our works. But we are not easily forgotten. Digging in the rich dark soil there are the folded fans of plastic wrappers, hard glass, oddments of vulcanised rubber. In parkland humans allow nature to flourish in a strictly controlled way. Here humanity, by clearing the land, has allowed nature to flourish ungoverned by our desires.

Standing in those wild, waste spaces I could feel the multiple layers. Like the soil, shot through with shredded bin liners. We are part of and yet so different from the rest of nature. We come and make our spaces, destroying to carve out our domains. But no sooner do we turn our back and all the little things; the creeping things, the crawling things, the tendril wavers and gossamer weavers, move back in. This was the transient chaos of these spaces. Beautiful, ghastly temporary autonomous zones. For me they simply stank, not only of dog piss and cow parsley, but of magick.

Green is the Colour

Blaise Castle was perhaps the first adult sized landscape that I developed a deep relationship with. Described, tongue in gothic cheek, by Jane Austen as 'the finest place in England' in her novel *Northanger Abbey*, Blaise sits on the northern edge of Bristol. Hundreds of acres of former mansion house estate are open to the public and it was here, during my late twenties, that I first really met the genius loci.

There are several gates. From my flat I could walk down the humdrum streets of the parish of Henbury, the bungalows peopled by an aged and delightfully quiet population. From here, cross the road and into the park. Through one gate a sward of lush grasses, fringed at the far end by dense trees. Here small human tracks criss-crossed the space. People meandering while their dogs skittered from fascinating scent to scent. A few impressive oaks, one lightning struck, a carbonised great God. Antlers spreading out in layers like coral shelves into the sky. Walk a little further, down to where the path begins. Again there are more choices. We can descend into the gorge that forms the heart of the estate or else skirt the houses that lie between the road and the grassland, and snake back toward the Church of St. Mary's.

Another route into this sacred space is to walk through the Churchyard. Crossing a stream by a narrow footway we emerge into the cemetery. The Church is an ancient low-slung building. Interred within its curtilage are the bones of black men and of wise women.

One gravestone, is dedicated to the memory of 'scipio Africanus' who was servant to Charles William, Earl of Suffolk and Bindon, who married one of the Astry family of Henbury House. The black servant was named after an ancient Roman general of African origin, Scipio Africanus. Scipio died in December 1720 at the age of 18. His is one of the most ornate graves in the Churchyard. The inscription of the memorial reads:

I who was Born a PAGAN and a SLAVE

Now Sweetly Sleep a CHRISTIAN in my Grave

What tho my hue was dark my SAVIORS sight

Shall Change this darkness into radiant light

Such grace to me my Lord on earth has given

To recommend me to my Lord in heaven

Whose glorious second coming here I wait

With saints and Angels Him to celebrate

Another liminal figure in this bone yard is that of Amelia Ann Blandford Edwards. This lady was an explorer, writer and Egyptologist. She founded the Chair of Egyptian Archaeology and Philology at University College London. She was also a determined campaigner against the looting of Ancient Egyptian antiquities. Upon her grave, close by the wall of the Church, is a beautiful obelisk and a large stone ankh resting on the earth. Symbols of eternal life and resurrection from that more ancient religion rubbing shoulders with Christian angels and deaths heads.

Blaise, so rich! So many walks and ways to explore it! I'd often give visitors that I was guiding through the gorge two choices. 'Would you like water and earth or fire and air?' If they chose the first we would walk down the valley, following an easy path. The 'beech cathedral' would be on our left. A stand of high trees on a steep but climbable slope. These tall queens of the forest sprang from knobbed and exposed roots, smoothed like beach pebbles by the run-off. Walking on downward, our next stop would be Goram's Chair. This vast double limestone outcrop (the arms of the seat) was the resting place of the giant Goram who made this gorge. He and the giant Vincent, who mined the Avon gorge, had a battle to see who was the stronger.

Legend has it that two local giants, Goram and Vincent - who, according to some versions were brothers - both had a bit of a thing for the same woman.

She was the lovely Avona, 'a Wiltshire-born merry belle' and promised to marry the first giant to drain the great lake that once stretched from Bradford-on-Avon to what is now Bristol.

Goram picked his route through Henbury Hills, while Vincent instead opted for Durdham Downs.

But the digging was thirsty work, and Goram soon succumbed to the heat, had a few pints and fell asleep in his favourite winged chair.

Meanwhile the ever-industrious Vincent furiously kept digging, emerging at Sea Mills, and duly won Avona's hand.

Avona gave her name to Vincent's Avon Gorge while Goram, who was broken hearted, hurled himself into the River Severn and drowned himself.

His head and shoulders can still be seen poking out of the estuary mud as the rocks of Flat Holm and Steep Holm, and his channel became known as the Hazel Brook gorge.

St Vincent's Rocks, near the Clifton Suspension Bridge, bear the name of the victor in this contest, but Goram is arguably more famous.

Giants moving on the land, making the places we little folk inhabit.

A little further down and we'd arrive at the giant's soap dish, a series of pools and ponds fed by the bright spilling hazel brook. For those who know there is an ancient oak hidden away in the forest at this spot. This great plant is hollow and one can stand inside, look up to the azure sky and hear the wind speaking doleful notes across the open tube of the trunk.

For a fire and air journey, we wind up the opposite side of the gorge. Here one encounters a low man-made cavern in the rock. Crouched inside this tiny space the ceiling is made from stones that point downwards, like the improbably numerous teeth of a shark. Up the hill, heaving in breath, getting closer and closer to the light. One might stop off and see Goram's footprint, an ancient depression in the rock (rather small given the prodigious size of his chair). Then darkness closes in as yew trees screen the gorge from view until one arrives, dizzy and gasping, to the look out. From this vantage point you can gaze out across the valley. Looking across the crowns of the trees and towards where the sun, in all her glory, is risen.

Turn the corner and you're at the famous folly celebrated by Austin. Folly is perhaps a misnomer since the structure was, until recently, inhabited and furnished in fabulous style (suits of armour, stags antlers on the walls, coats of arms and rich floor rugs). The building is, as any 5 year old will tell you, a castle. Crenulated towers stand proud on a close-cropped lawn. We may go one way and down towards the giant sequoia, with its strange fibrous red bark, and back to the manor house. Alternatively one might turn and walk along out past another stand of trees and along the ridge where the ancient Roman sun temple once stood. It was on a walk that took such a route that I met Pan.

Many of my walks on Blaise were in company, sometimes alone, many times with my allies. At that period of my life these were typically LSD and cannabis. A typical practice would include nothing more elaborate than making some simple prayers, taking the acid and meditating until I (or we) could feel it coming on. Then we'd go outside to trip. To make the psychedelic journey linked, enhanced by, the actual journey through a fairly safe certainly very beautiful landscape.

But the time I saw Pan I'd not taken acid, although it's probable I'd been smoking weed, this was relatively sober vision.

I'd gone for a walk, just because it was a gorgeous day. High summer with that full deep green, not yet tipping into the dusty gold of early autumn. I walked up the path of fire and air, paid my respects at the Castle and then set off to look for the Iron Age mound on the ridge. This structure can be seen easily, since the land is a field of grasses with only a few hawthorns dotted here and there. The low mound overlooks Avonmouth and it was on this hill that the Romans placed their solar shrine. Standing in some oak woods looking across the grassland I exclaimed to myself 'well if there is a Lord of the Forest, this is where he'd be'. The God I imagined was the strong, vigorous deity of the sun, the oak king, the bright jocund Emperor of Summer.

As I turned around there, sitting on a fallen oak, was a man. He was dressed in a dishevelled suit that was of indeterminate age. He wore a bowler hat and had a purple necktie. What was odd, and I only had a few moments to notice it, was that his suit, indeed all of him, was green.

"It's a beautiful day". He said with a slight Irish accent.

Stuck by his silent arrival I simply smiled and nodded.

"Ah well, you go your way and I'll go mine." He said, and winked.

I turned my attention for a moment back to the grasses swaying on the field. Of course when I turned back he had gone.

I looked round for him. There was only one easily accessible path and he didn't look the athletic type, but he was nowhere to be seen.

Was this figure a spirit? Perhaps my Green Man of the woods? Or was he nothing more than a Falstaffian tramp, a gentleman of the road who'd stopped to take a breather in the shade of the woods? Was he the jolly incarnation of Pan, more *Wind In The Willows* than the rampaging deity of Crowley's famous invocation? There was a gust of wind and a distinct sense of the sacred.

With the miracle medicine of LSD inside me I'd seen many signs that pointed to the power in that landscape. The washing in an out of the trees, standing proud on the ridges of the limestone gorge. I'd watched the crows flying across the dawn chasing the pale departure of the full moon as the sun swept up into the sky. I'd watched, as my friend Richard became a leaping lion in the moonlight, aboriginal markings on his face reminding me of the antipodean continent he was visiting me from. I'd felt my body electrified with energy, scrambling a screen slope of the valley, and seen the hair of a beautiful woman merge with the yew tree in which she sat. But never had I experienced such a commonplace, defiantly real and yet mysterious encounter as with that green man. That was a special blessing from that landscape that I'd fallen in love with.

Going West

Since moving to north Devon I've had many opportunities to get to know the countryside of the most southwestern part of Britain. Frequently these journeys have been in the company of Greg Humphries my dear friend, magical collaborator and sometime co-author. Together we've walked the landscape of Cornwall, infested with Neolithic monuments and the echoes of miners' hammers. We've delved into coombes, those special deep wooded valleys, of north Devon. Together we improvised and deployed a range of different techniques for engaging with the spirit of the land. Here are a few examples;

Shrine Making

Found objects and those brought along expressly for the purpose can be used to honour the local spirits. Shrines are built, little altars dressed with flowers, coloured wool, trinkets, and offerings of money and joints. Such interventions serve to mark our sacred attention to the landscape and leave a trail of ritual that, I hope, enhances the journey of those who subsequently discover them. Tiny transient mementoes of meditations that punctuate the ritual walk.

On fences ribbons may be tied, grasses woven with spells through the mesh, and feathers stuck in the cracks between brickwork. Our magick seeks out these crevices in the works of man, unstoppable and temporary as a mushroom that pushes out of the gap between paving slabs.

Offerings

A shrine is a species of offering, a marking not of territory but of sacredness. Offerings can also be made to gatekeepers and sacred spots. Candles are left at wells along with silver coins (and wishes). Blood may need to be spilt or tobaccos placed under the earth.

Artworks

Inspired by Andy Goldsworthy leaves can be laid in a line. Graduations of colour, from green to autumn reds mark this out as the work of man. The large rounded grey pebbles of the north Devon coast can be arranged so that the veins of quartz crystals within them line up. These bright white lines snake across the beach, creating an order that is distinctly human. Or they may be piled up, balanced on top of each other (I once saw a beach on the isle of Agnes in the Scilly's that had hundreds of such piles, a sculptured landscape).

Drawing and painting on surfaces, on abandoned signs, on great rocks, can also be a way of honouring the spirit of place. (Although I usually content myself with chalk rather than spray paint.)

Right Way of Walking

The terrain offers many ways of locomotion. Walking up a hill, head down looking just a few feet ahead, against the solid wind. Then looking down from a high place once a vantage point is attained. In this way we go from the view of the mouse to that of the hawk. Once Greg and I climbed a slope covered in heathers and moss. Like lovers pawing over the luxurious hair on the vaginal mound of a huge Goddess. Sniffing her, feeling her wiry fur. So absorbed were we in this erotic close contact that it was only when the ground ran out we realised we'd climbed a huge sea cliff. Over the sharp edge was the glittering ocean and bright air.

Then there is the part of the walk that is real Work. The interminable slog back to the car along the unrelenting metalled road. The final push to get to the peak before we can rest and take it all in. Walking can be a challenging business.

Entheogens

Taken inside entheogens tend towards introspection or a shared group consciousness if used as part of a collective ceremony. Outside they allow us to see the fantastic beauty of nature through fresh eyes. We slow down; take everything in. Tuffs of dune grass blowing in the sun become the tousled air of bleached blond surfers. Rivers are seen and known as the veins of the planet. Birds become messengers from other worlds. We see in a way that is both hyper-symbolised and yet somehow also shorn of preconceptions. We focus on those aspects of the land that have something to teach us. I spent one journey obsessed by 'the edge', the razor cut sheering away of cliffs. The point at which the sea and the land and sky all meet. Entheogens adjust our perception so that we are seeing the liminal, the within and the without, as they meet.

Of course one must judge the dose well, especially if interaction with other people or negotiating dangerous landscapes is required. However legal and safety considerations aside LSD, mushrooms and other typtamines are wonderful spirits to go walking with. As one commentator put it:

> But they (drugs) all do sort of the same thing, and that is rearrange what you thought was real, and they remind you of the beauty of pretty simple things. You forget, because you're so busy going from A to Z, that there's 24 letters in between...

The term 'museum level' has been used to describe the dose of a psychoactive where one might be able to function in a social space (for example a visit to a gallery or cream-tea shop) and not be so wired that you get thrown out (or become reduced to a paranoid wreck). Such a level of intoxication is ideal for walking. One can also use the shorter acting substances (for example smoked DMTs) at the literal peak of a journey. Clearly one should find a safe environment within which to take these substances since they can be temporarily incapacitating. Proximity to cliffs and mine shafts is to be avoided!

Song and sound

Another archaic technique of ecstasy. Whether it be listening hard to the sound of your own feet on the earth, humming or singing as one walks, or perhaps using mantra and vibrated words of power at stops along the route. Making sounds we contribute to the soundscape of a place. By inducing trance, rhythmic sound can help us to focus deeply on one aspect of a location (playing with echoes and percussive sounds is an excellent way to do this). As we become ecstatic, literally standing outside of ourselves, our perspective can shift. We are no longer beings walking on the land, instead we are in it and of it.

Prayer and words of power can be spoken at sacred locations; lone trees, crossroads, bridges. We can program ourselves with spelling, sounding out our intentions as we send driftwood wands out to sea, or touch sacred objects; megaliths, doorways, windmills.

It's good to save words at some points in a magical walk. Make times when chitchat is minimised. Walk in silence and only say when you are moved to do so by deep unconscious forces. Make sounds in reply to the wind and talk to the animals and plants with respectful, measured dialogue. This way the act of speaking is potentiated. Listening is also enhanced this way. And if there is conversation it should be remembered that this is as special space and words should be chosen with flare and care.

Hiding Things

Talismans, witch bottles, runes and tokens can be buried and secreted along the journey. These act as gnostic strange attractors, linking your power to the place you have visited.

Eating and Drinking

It's possible, even on an urban walk in all but the most densely populated areas, to find wild foods to eat. Seaweeds, blackberries, the cucumbery taste of fleshy navelwort, the coconut dryness of gorse flowers. Literally eating the landscape it becomes you. Drinking from a stream where the water is fresh, tasting the brine of the sea. Getting all gustatory with the planet is good for the mind, body and soul. It also leaves you with a nice feeling that if the total breakdown of civilisation happens anytime soon you'll be able to survive, for a while at least.

Naturally this is an incomplete list. The key is to listen to the place, the space, and respond to it. If that means silent meditation do it. If that means breath work or bathing in the sea, let it happen. Watch how watercourses move, if they are flowing away from you ask them to help you banish restrictions. If towards you ask them to bring you insights and divinations. Listen to the earth, press your ear down on the soil and really strain to hear. Is it speaking? What does it say?

And built environments of course present their own opportunities. Watch for omens in pub signs and random graffiti. Deploy your mobile phone and exchange pictures with confederates who are walking at the same time but in different locations. (Mobile phones incidentally also provide a social cover for techniques such as glossolalia. One can burble into a state of trance with a mobile held to the ear and thus appear to be speaking a curious language rather than being certifiably insane.) In cities one can make the classic situationist dérive or 'dift', moving through passageways that you've never investigated before, back alleys of the towns that are analogous to the half-hidden routes through your own unconscious mind. Ivan Chtcheglov, writing in a letter to Guy Debord in 1963 says; *"The dérive (with its flow of acts, its gestures, its strolls, its encounters) was to the totality exactly what psychoanalysis (in the best sense) is to language. Let yourself go with the flow of words, says the psychoanalyst. He listens, until the moment when he rejects or modifies (one could say detourns) a word, an expression or a definition. The dérive is certainly a technique, almost a therapeutic one."*

For the within is alike the without. We realise ourselves as beings congruent with the perception the Tralfamadorian aliens have of us in Kurt Vonnegut's novel *Slaughterhouse 5*. At our tail is a birthing babe, our head is a bloated corpse. But between these points, in innumerable centipede like segments, our histories coil around the earth.

Let us make these movements of our journey full of pleasure and freedom and power. Let us be inspired by the spirits of place, work with them, honour them and see ourselves in relationship with all those things that share our world. Let's explore this territory like astronauts on a new planet, or toddlers discovering for the first time how it feels to walk on warm sand. Let's disorientate ourselves with chanting and drifting, with drugs and art. And in this disorientation we pray for a new connection, a re-enchantment of the land and our place within it.

Pull back; see the setting sun not as the orb of light going down, but as the planet turning at hundreds of miles per hour in space. Glance down; and watch the tiny spider sucking the life out of her captives, these myriad transformations on every scale. By these acts, these shifts of perception, this relationship we make with the earth, we expose the magick in all manifest existence. So it goes.

The Three Schools of Magick – by Way of Introduction

An essay apropos of nothing at all

Crowley famously said there were three types of magician. The Black, Yellow and White Schools. These are three philosophical positions that boil down to styles of engagement with the world. They each approach the 'problem' of reality from different perspectives, which in some senses are complementary.

It is in *Magick Without Tears* that Crowley really develops this idea that locks right into his first obsession – the notion of a body of Secret Chiefs. The Occult Illuminati who are the guardians of the inestimable treasures of arcane knowledge. The real power behind many of the social and political events of human history. This Elite Unseen University, this Invisible College, was a central conceit of the Hermetic Order of the Golden Dawn. Contact with mysterious initiates is the stock-in-trade of many magickal lineages.

The tripartite division of this College is something Crowley alludes to in his Enochian vision of the aethyr called MAZ. Here he sees three adepts moving in the astral mindscape in relation to 'the Most High'. The Black Adept walks forwards, the White backwards and the Yellow to one side. This kinaesthetic teaching is mirrored in the essential differences between the Schools. Crowley defines these schools in *Magick Without Tears* thus;

Yellow

The Yellow School of Magick considers, with complete scientific and philosophical detachment, the fact of the Universe as a fact. Being itself apart of that Universe, it realizes its impotence to alter the totality in the smallest degree. To put it vulgarly, it does not try to raise itself from the ground by pulling at its socks. It therefore opposes to the current of phenomena no reaction either of hatred or of sympathy. So far as it attempts to influence the course of events at all, it does so in the only intelligent way conceivable. It seeks to diminish internal friction.

Black

The analysis of the philosophers of this School refers every phenomenon to the category of sorrow. It is quite useless to point out to them that certain events are accompanied with joy: they continue their ruthless calculations, and prove to your satisfaction, or rather dissatisfaction, that the more apparently pleasant an event is, the more malignantly deceptive is its fascination. There is only one way of escape even conceivable, and this way is quite simple, annihilation.

White

Existence is pure joy. Sorrow is caused by failure to perceive this fact; but this is not a misfortune. We have invented sorrow, which does not matter so much after all, in order to have the exuberant satisfaction of getting rid of it. Existence is thus a sacrament.

When using the Crowleyian nomenclature we fall immediately into the problem of having to distinguish between the terms Black Brother (what I refer to as a 'Bloodless Adept' – see *Magick Works*) and Black School. A Black Brother, in a nutshell, is someone who seeks to isolate himself or herself from the evolutionary flow of the universe. Some left hand path systems include this approach overtly but Black Brothers also turn up in the right-handed styles. A Black Brother seeks to maintain their Self against the universal process of change or, as they would probably see it, decay.

The Black School is not the same as Black Brotherhood. Neither is 'black' in the sense of 'wrong' or evil. (Indeed one would be hard pressed to affirm that even the Black Brothers work is necessarily 'evil' in all senses of the word.) Neither is it the case that the White School are the goodies (or goodie-two-shoes) in the story. The Three Schools are simply three approaches. But the classification provided by Crowley is clumsy. Therefore Soror Lilavirananda and I have proposed the following revised schema viz;

The Tigger School – the equivalent of the White School.

The Eeyore School – formerly the Black School.

The Pooh School – previously the Yellow School.

The Three Schools are mostly clearly understood in terms of the initiation of Binah, the Master or Mistress of the Temple within the scheme developed by the Hermetic Order of The Golden Dawn. In this grade the magician takes their seat in the City of Pyramids under the Night of Pan. The magician also begins to care for the neophytes as the gardener of souls.

So how does our revised terminology fit the philosophies of the Three Schools? Drawing from the writings of A.A.Milne, let us begin our analysis with the School that includes much of Hindu and monotheist philosophies;

Eeyore, the old grey Donkey, stood by the side of the stream, and looked at himself in the water.

> "Pathetic," he said. "That's what it is. Pathetic."

He turned and walked slowly down the stream for twenty yards, splashed across it, and walked slowly back on the other side. Then he looked at himself in the water again.

> "As I thought," he said. "No better from this side. But nobody minds. Nobody cares. Pathetic, that's what it is."

Eeyore does not differentiate one side of the river from the other. It's all the same to him. For members of the Eeyore School maintaining equanimity in the face of any given circumstance is the aim. It is the impermanence of existence that inspires Eeyore. And he recognises that it is our attachment to the constantly shifting forms of the universe that creates suffering.

> "After all, what are birthdays? Here today and gone tomorrow."

Yet the Eeyore School is not without its humour, albeit of the gallows variety. Indeed this dark humour points towards laughter (which can be malevolent or magnanimous), the Trance of Laughter that unites all three Schools.

"It's snowing still," said Eeyore gloomily.

"So it is."

"And freezing."

"Is it?"

"Yes," said Eeyore. "However," he said, brightening up a little, "we haven't had an earthquake lately."

"And any one of the movements of the mind is (with assiduity and enthusiasm) capable of transforming the Trance of Sorrow itself into the cognate Trance attributed to Understanding, the Trance of Wonder." So Crowley writes in his *Little Essays Towards Truth*. From Eeyore's Trance of Sorrow, Tigger leads us into the Trance of Wonder.

Of course from the perspective of Eeyore Tigger seems like a vacuous or even degenerate animal.

Eeyore walked all round Tigger one way, and then turned and walked round him the other way.

"What did you say it was?" he asked.

"Tigger."

"Ah!" said Eeyore.

"He's just come," explained Piglet.

"Ah!" said Eeyore again.

He thought for a long time and then said: "When is he going?"

Arriving in the middle of the night in *The House at Pooh Corner*, Tigger is hungry. He claims to like 'everything', but experiment demonstrates that he really doesn't care for honey, acorns or thistles. What we can be certain about with Tigger is that he is a literally larger than life character. He is force and fire and form.

And the Small and Sorry Rabbit rushed through the mist at the noise, and it suddenly turned into Tigger; a Friendly Tigger, a Grand Tigger, a Large and Helpful Tigger, a Tigger who bounced, if he bounced at all, in just the beautiful way a Tigger ought to bounce.

Piglet was still a little anxious about Tigger, who was a very Bouncy Animal, with a way of saying How-do-you-do, which always left your ears full of sand, even after Kanga had said "Gently, Tigger dear," and had helped you up again.

Tigger does not recognise his own preferences and limitations. He shows little or no restraint and in some respects does not appear to know himself very well. However one might also say that Tigger is fully open to the possibilities of the universe and sees each engagement with reality as a superlative opportunity. The central activity of Tigger is 'to bounce'. This activity underscores Tigger's quality of plasticity and movement. He is the dynamic, desirous force of the universe. As a species of Tiger our striped guru represents individualism and ferocious desire, *carpe diem* might well be his motto. His style reminds us of the injunction from *The Book of the Law*:

> "Remember all ye that existence is pure joy: that all the sorrows are but as shadows; they pass & are done; but there is that which remains."

The bounce, that joyous springtime leap is emblematic of the frenzy of desire. This remains even after the sorrows (Tigger's rejection of acorns, honey and thistles) are done.

Unlike Eeyore, Pooh is able to develop a good relationship with Tigger despite his intensely effervescent style;

> "Tigger is all right, really," said Pooh lazily.
>
> "Of course he is," said Christopher Robin.
>
> "Everybody is really," said Pooh. "That's what I think," said Pooh. "But I don't suppose I'm right," he said.
>
> "Of course you are," said Christopher Robin.

As a Taoist, Pooh believes that it is a return to the original simplicity that brings with it wisdom.

> "Sometimes, if you stand on the bottom rail of a bridge and lean over to watch the river slipping slowly away beneath you, you will suddenly know everything there is to be known."

In common with many Taoist thinkers it is the relationship between the Self and Nature that is central to Pooh's philosophy. ("Rivers know this: there is no hurry. We shall get there some day.") He also recognises that the day-to-day life of the domestic sphere is as likely to lead to spiritual awakening as anything else;

> "When you wake up in the morning, Pooh," said Piglet at last, "what's the first thing you say to yourself?"
>
> "What's for breakfast?" said Pooh. "What do you say, Piglet?"
>
> "I say, I wonder what's going to happen exciting today?" said Piglet.
>
> Pooh nodded thoughtfully.
>
> "It's the same thing," he said.

The element of worldly simplicity is strong in much Taoist thinking. Taoist teachers will often discuss their philosophy in terms of sex, death and money since these are common concepts rather than relying on complex metaphysics (although the core elements of Taoism by their very nature are subtle in the extreme). Pooh expressed this insight thus:

> "It is more fun to talk with someone who doesn't use long, difficult words but rather short, easy words like 'What about lunch?' "

Like the supremely economic movements of a Tai chi form each act naturally follows the next. It is this 'obvious' realisation of the nature of things that Pooh cultivates:

> "When looking at your two paws, as soon as you have decided which of them is the right one, then you can be sure the other one is the left."

Can we extend this approach? Does the adept (the Magus) aim to be like Christopher Robin, or even perhaps Piglet? Undoubtedly there is great value in the works of A.A.Milne, which should certainly be studied by all serious students of the Qabalah and those dedicated to The Great Work of Magick. If nothing else we should be mindful of the curious resemblance between Milne and the Discordian Reverend Bob Dobbs. Are they perchance related? Perhaps we should be told...

Fig 3 A.A.Milne & The Reverend Bob Dobbs

Baphomet Rising

> Observe for yourselves the decay of the sense of sin, the growth of innocence and irresponsibility, the strange modifications of the reproductive instinct with a tendency to become bi-sexual or epicene,
>
> Aleister Crowley, *The Book of Thoth*

> I first heard of this bloke, this fucking rumour going round
> Your mother's reputation it's not sound
> She's saving up the pennies hoping they'd turn into pounds
> To have an operation to swap her gender around.
>
> Goldie Looking Chain, *Your Mother's Got A Penis*

There are certain key zones of power in any culture, places where the walls of consensus reality are rather thin. It is at these places that magicians like to detonate charges of gnosis, detonations that allow different aspects of reality to rupture and mingle. There are of course many reasons for these deeds. To the 'straight' world this can appear as nothing more than wicked behaviour, upsetting the applecart of reality just for the hell of it. Sometimes these detonations are about smashing the fetters of what is 'normal', revealing that much of what oppresses us are our own mind-forged manacles (as Blake brilliantly describes them). Then there are times, or aspects of these detonations, which have transpersonal even Aeonic meanings and effects. One such detonation is that which takes place in the interface between the worlds of gender identity and sexuality.

Of course many cultures admit a range of gender and sexual styles. Even within the dominant patriarchal religions and cultures on our planet, acceptance, formal or otherwise, of lesbianism, celibacy, homosexuality and other sexual styles does exist. However acceptance of these behaviours is typically at a cultural (ie pragmatic day-to-day level) rather than something that holy writ promotes. In some cultures, notably the more diverse and tolerant forms of Hinduism, sexual and gender flexibility is somewhat greater. The Hijra cultures of South Asia include people who are male, female or intersex. Frequently they dress as women but regard themselves as a third sex. There are parallels with the role of the berdache (or perhaps more politically correctly 'two-spirit') people of Native American cultures, who are typically also considered a third sex or a blend of both genders in one individual.

There are, of course, plenty of exemplars of gender and sexual polymorphism in contemporary tribal cultures and in the mythology of pre-monotheist Europe and Asia. Even within the superficially macho world of North West European Paganism we have the character of Odin whom some representations depict with both male and female characteristics, as well as that tell-tell mutilated left eye. Although one might critique the image of the bisexual shaman as a modern liberal reading of ancient texts, there are, I feel, sufficient examples of this complex to testify to its reality. The liminality of the shaman, or perhaps simply the neurology of those attracted to that social role, leads to gender and sexual fluidity.

A quick ethnography of modern occultists serves to back this up. Aleister Crowley was bisexual and quite liked dressing up in women's clothing and trying to seduce his students. Austin Spare enjoyed a range of exotic magickal masturbatory methods and was partial to shagging elderly women and orgiastic dreamworld excursions. Political radical and Goddess feminist Zsuzsanna Budapest was married with children but then divorced and identified herself as lesbian. Genesis P.Orridge and Oryelle Defenestrate-Bascule have both explored physical alteration of their bodies in order to destabilise their apparent gender as men. The list goes on. In fact it's probably the case that we should ask 'how many occultists are really straight?' There are of course people such as Dion Fortune, who certainly appears to have been fairly 'conventionally' monogamous and heterosexual. But even in these cases the occultist still recognises the interwoven forces of sexuality and gender as constituting one of the critical zones of magickal power. Fortune calls this 'polarity' and her theorisations about this interplay of forces, is central in Wicca and also Druidry.

Of course there are lots of folk who are led into the world of polymorphous sexuality simply because of how they feel. The frequently quoted idea of being 'a woman in a man's body' (or vice versa) is certainly true for some people. Still others are seeking to re-define their sexuality in ways that are less about a clear identification with any given gender role or sexual preference. 'Pansexual' (which I think is a great word for all the obvious reasons), 'polyamourous', 'fluid' or 'ethical slutdom', are terms that have been created to meet this need.

The emergence of this playful sexual experimentation is a function of the psycho-historical process that Crowley called the emergence of the Aeon of The Child. Hence his quote at the start of this essay. The world inhabited by magicians is not, of course, divorced from the rest of culture. In some ways magicians can be the trailblazers; deliberately exploring sexuality and gender in ritual and other practices. In another sense magick, like art, reflects those transformations of society that emerge from the deepest currents of human evolution.

The modern age has also seen a variety of practical techniques that can facilitate this kind of exploration. From full gender reassignment surgery, through to ear piercing and long hair, there is now both a tolerance (in many places in the Western world) for a range of styles of display. Sure you're still likely to get the shit kicked out of you if you're a man dressed as a woman out in a homophobic part of the world, but there is an increasing range and number of spaces (including public spaces) where you might get away with it.

Surgical and hormonal modification has opened up a vast range of possibilities. Fancy having a completely new set of genitalia? What about a nice pair of breast implants? Then there has been the investigation of archaic methods of body modification and the rejuvenation of these in the modern age.

These practices arise into a multiplicity of forms, and indeed some techniques can be deployed several times by one individual. Whereas once our mechanisms for gender exploration relied on clothing, padding and strapping the body into new configurations, now we can use surgeon's blades and hormones to affect even deeper levels of transformation. Thus our planet now plays host to a wide variety of beings who embody the dual gender and which previously has been the preserve only of mythological figures.

The T-girl, shemale, transvestite, ladyboy, transsexual et al are emerging from the broom closet and into wider culture. The present emo generation sports a clear sexual ambiguity reminiscent of David Bowie's Ziggy Stardust (though in the case of emo kids that trademark mullet is worn backwards). From the kink culture of *Rocky Horror* to the dance floor of the Torture Garden, cross-dressing and transgressions of gender identity are becoming more and more frequent.

These social changes are part of the arising of the force I identify as Baphomet. In one sense Baphomet is the life force, and therefore specifically the sexual energy, of the planet. Moreover Baphomet is the divine androgyny, possessed of phallus and delicious tits. But perhaps most important of all, Baphomet is the gnostic process, the direct exploration of the world as the means to divine knowledge. Rather than place our authority in sacred texts, Baphomet is the process whereby, through experiment, the self becomes aware of the universe. DNA sits up and realises its own structure in biology, mind awakens and understands itself through neurology and psychology. Sexuality finds itself in a free, unrestricted space and can explore and evolve. For many people on the earth, challenges to the authority of priests and mullahs and politicians (as arbiters of what is right in the case of sexual conduct), are gaining ground. Rather than see our sexual identity only in terms of conventional interpretations of monotheist scripture, we realise that we must discover this identity for ourselves.

This spirit of playfulness, the Child-like quality of Crowley's Horus Aeon (or the playful Pan-esque vibe of Baphomet), is essential in sexual discovery. No longer do most of us tell our children that 'playing with themselves' will lead to Hell and damnation. Instead increasing numbers of people have normalised and accepted behaviours that, for thousands of years, have been taboo. The vast change in the cultural position of homosexuality is a great case in point, outlawed for hundreds of years there has been a massive global shift in its legal status in many nations.

Indeed homosexuality is now so well accepted as 'normal' that organisations such as Amnesty International campaign for gay rights as equivalent to human rights. When we consider that this cultural change has occurred against the backdrop of most major religions believing that homosexuality is sinful, this is a truly revolutionary situation. (Perhaps in time Amnesty will also be campaigning on behalf of prisoners who are incarcerated because of their use of entheogens?)

More and more of us are being born into an existential world, a world in which there is much less in the way of explicit script than there was in the past. We are fluid, we are philosophers finding our own way, certainly informed and influenced by other people, but hungry to make our own discoveries and to locate our own path. In terms of sexuality this process of discovery is perhaps best arrived at as play. Role-play, sex play, deep play – whatever we call it. Rather than fixate on our identity as straight, queer, leather-daddy, butch or whatever many people are seeking instead places (both physical and psychological) where sexuality can be played with. Once more this is that gnostic Baphometic drive, the need to experiment for oneself, rather than adopting an off-the-peg, specific sexual identity. And even where identity is important, for example in terms of claiming cultural space in the way that gay men have done, people are increasingly aware that identity itself can be fuzzy, fluid and temporary.

The emergence and maintenance of environments such as the swingers bar, the kinky party, the chaos magick temple, the polyamory conference – these and many other locations are the incubation chambers for Baphomet. The proliferation of erotic forms, a bouquet of sexual possibilities, constellations of mouths and hands and cunts and cocks – these are the nurseries of the new sexuality.

Of course we should not rest on our laurels. There are still many, many places on our planet where this sexuality fluidity and exploration is not permitted. There is so much we need, as a culture, to learn about the methods of safe, respectful and empowering sexual exploration. Support systems need to be enshrined in culture and in law to support these investigations, and we need more and deeper acceptance of the panchromatic nature of human sexuality. We also need to address the shadow of this sexual revolution. The horror with which paedophilia is greeted in our society is perhaps the reflexive form of increasing sexual tolerance. We need to investigate ways of understanding consent, culpability and sexual power. We need to look closely at how powerfully the mob scapegoating behaviour is engendered by cries of 'paedo!' We need to teach our children to enjoy and reverence their sexuality; we need to appreciate where sexual abuse really happens (mostly in families and very rarely by random sinister strangers). We need to protect our young from sexual violence but not fall into the trap of believing that they are not themselves sexual beings.

But the prize for such challenging work is a great one. From sexuality flows pleasure, flows ecstasy. This personal cultivation of ecstasy is the magick of the new aeon. As easily experienced with stockings and a nice kangaroo leather flogger as it is with a copy of *Liber AL* and ceremonial robes. And as we open, as a society, as a species to this pansexual impulse we are invoking Baphomet as joyous rapture of the earth. Filling us up with love, with desire, with comfort and with care. Making us realise that our sexuality is a field of experience, a garden within which this God wishes us to explore and delight.

The Mass of Abraxas

A ritual featuring a giant golden egg, a chicken mask and a gentleman with a pipe.

This ritual forms part of the Baphomet Work that Soror Res and members of the Western Watchtower have developed.

The ritual comes in two parts. The first is an elemental healing rite developed by Frater Pelagius the second part occurs outside and has been developed by Frater Pelagius & Frater Salar.

Preamble and health and safety information concerning the Foxy sacrament for this rite.

Section One – Elemental Healing.

The elemental weapons are placed on the ground.

IAO banishing.

Abraxas invocation by Frater Salar over sacrament capsules. These are administered in silence.

Frater Pelagius provides an introduction to the practice;

Large sheets of paper, one for each of the four elements, are placed on the ground. Using pens participants write down words that they associate with each element.

Continue in this way until all are done.

Each person then picks an element that they feel they need to open up to more fully.

Participants pair up and provide healing for each other; this may be done using mantra, massage or other methods. Pairs then reverse roles, the healer becomes the healed.

A bell is rung to signal the end of this section of the ritual.

A moment of silence.

Everyone disrobes and puts on boots.

When all are ready Frater Pelagius leads participants out to the roundhouse to the beat of the drum.

Section Two – Dance of Abraxas

In the roundhouse a fire has been prepared and lit. Officers now station themselves at the four directions.

East – smudge.

South – fire (with iron filings/sugar to throw in the flames)

West – an aspergillum and water

North – Drum.

Participants hold hands, and begin to circle around. As they go by each station they receive the blessing of that element. Once all are blessed the officers join the circle.

Frater Serpents Columba stands in the centre of the circle. He holds in his hands the mask of Abraxas. He begins the invocation.

"Abraxas speaketh that hallowed and accursed word which is life and death at the same time. Abraxas begetteth truth and lying, good and evil, light and darkness in the same word and in the same act. Wherefore is Abraxas terrible."

"IO IO IO IAO SABAO KURIE ABRASAX KURIE MEITHRAS KURIE PHALLE. IO PAN, IO PAN PAN IO ISCHUROS, IO ATHANATOS IO ABROTOS IO IAO. KAIRE PHALLE KAIRE PAMPHAGE KAIRE PANGENETOR. HAGIOS, HAGIOS, HAGIOS IAO."

"The bird fights its way out of the egg. The egg is the world. Who would be born must destroy a world. The bird flies to God. That God's name is Abraxas."

The drummer leaves the circle and continues to play. The person who has already been selected to lead the dance puts on the mask and begins to lead the dance out of the roundhouse and into the woodland.

As the party leave one of the officers returns to the temple and moves the egg, on a cloth, to the centre of the space.

After a suitable period of woodland frolics the leader of the dance leads the snake back inside the roundhouse.

The leader of the dance comes to stand over the golden egg. Others circle the space.

Frater Serpents Columba says

"If the chick cannot break the shell of its egg, it will die without being born. We are the chick; the world is our egg. If we cannot break the world's shell, we will die without being born. Smash the world's shell - for the revolution of the world!"

Participants then make unearthly cockerel and chicken style noises. The egg is cracked open.

Banish with Clucking.

Fig 4 Abraxas

The mask was easy. After taking coffee with Frater Pelagius we were walking past a theatrical costumier. There in the window was a full head, yellow chicken mask. Clearly a sign! Manufacturing the egg took a lot longer. Layers of flour and water paste, laying strips of paper over a gigantic balloon. Slowly building up the layers and doing so while much of my life fell apart. The whole process took several weeks, with periods of drying required between the layers. I recall dipping the newspaper strips in the glue, fixing them criss-cross over the egg shaped form. High on ecstasy and yet weeping, hot lonely tears. But then again I don't suppose making an egg is exactly pleasurable for a hen, so I'm not complaining.

By the day of the ritual the egg was completed. Two feet high, painted gold with sparkling golden spirals drawn over its surface. Inside we placed sweets; gelatine serpents, liquorish capsules of many different colours, lurid green chewy bars in coloured wrappers bearing the legend 'toxic Waste!'

The night of the ritual came. Our traditional early summer ritual space with purpose built low impact temple space and outdoor roundhouse. The sacrament was a novel one for most participants, so I erred on the side of scarcity. In ritual work less is typically more, and with a new material one needs to be careful. One untypical reaction could easily put a real downer on the party (and we were several miles from the nearest medical facility).

The bird has flown, the egg an empty shell.

Into a new world we arise.

The Ketacean Kundalini Kult

The Initiatory Work of Temple K

I've been tracking this group for some time now and finally I think I've got enough material to create if not the full story then at least part of it. The 'K-OS' or 'temple K', as they usually refer to themselves, is a transmission, a current rather than an exclusive group. Its membership seems to include people involved in a number of esoteric orders and different occult paths but the ritual style (especially the iconography and process of the initiation rite I'm about to describe) appears to be common to all the 'cult' cells.

Each group consists of at least three members. The triangle forms one of the key symbols of this group and this image, like most of the technology the group uses, is derived from messages received through the use of their entheogenic sacrament – ketamine.

The three members of each cell (or sometimes 'node' or 'nest') are the doorways through which new initiates pass. I can describe the initiation ritual itself in some detail as I've just passed through that portal and become a member myself.

The ritual itself is a classic death and rebirth, the standard sort of procedure that occurs in most religious systems. The practicalities of the ritual are as follows.

The setting can be wildly variable but generally a warm comfortable indoor space is chosen. Blankets, furry cushions and mattresses are the order of the day. The ritual begins with the sharing of water. The water itself is said to contain water preserved from previous ceremonies. In this way the group aim to carry something of the power of each ritual through into the next, building higher and higher levels of esoteric power, like a charge being built up in a battery. Water is the sacred relic of the K-OS.

Water is placed in a vessel (usually a glass cup) and a prayer is said over it. Although there are no fixed words for the ceremony this is what happened the night I attended. There were three others present. I'll call them X, Y and Z.

We sat together and Z held his hands towards the water.

"This is the water of life. This is the water of life. This is the water of life".

We all repeated this statement.

Z said "All good spirits are here. All helpful forces. All beings are friendly to each other in this space". Softly X and Y added their statements, along the same lines but not exactly the same words, to this prayer.

"This is the water of life" (Again chanted three times).

Z said, "All is good here, all are well and strong". Again X and Y echoed the sentiment that we were all whole and strong.

"This is the water of life" (Again chanted three time).

This time Z raised his voice. "We are explorers, evolving, mutating and changing", again X and Y added their words to this prayer. "We are magickians, we dare to develop and to grow".

We took a sip of the water each, in silence. Then the central act of the ceremony begins.

Imagine being cocooned. Wrapped up tightly in grey-black coloured cling film.

It begins at the ankles. Legs are bound tightly together. Hands down by the sides, in turn captured and pinned down. The ripping sound of the film as sections are tied round the body, the person doing the mummification occasionally twisting the roll to create areas of increased tension.

The wrapping is like a death shroud. The plastic is tight, though the person wrapping you takes care to ensure that you can breathe (the face is initially exposed, the tension of the film is reduced around the neck). Finally the plastic covers the whole form with the exception of the head. That is when they ask you:

"Do you Julian Sebastian Vayne wish to make the journey?" X asks.

(This is the last chance.)

"Yes!"

X demands, "Do you absolve us of all responsibility for whatever happens to you?"

"Yes!"

Then she holds up the mirror. I think: "I know this person. I've come to trust her. I've come to trust the two men who are standing behind me, steadying my now wavering body."

She holds a bank note (perhaps a dollar bill?) up my left nostril. On the mirror are several lines of ketamine, three small doses for the other members of this strange gathering and one big one. For me.

I determinedly snort half the line. The tube is inserted in my right nostril and I inhale the rest. The curious relationship between this practice and ancient Egyptian mummification (where the brain of the deceased is removed through the nostrils) pops into my mind. Then the sound starts again. The ripping of cling film as my face is covered. What seems like layer and layer is added until I cannot see. Although I don't hear it I know (or hope) that the hourglass (another central symbol of the cult) has been inverted. The sand pours through, marking time by the creation of a tiny pyramid of sand. I hope this device is running and will be attended to. Since my companions are also taking doses of ketamine (though their doses are about a third of mine) and they need to keep it together while I am in this vulnerable state.

Then there is a moment of panic, welling up from deep inside. Oh my God! Perhaps this is it! Perhaps these people are really crazy! Perhaps they mean to kill me! I realise how completely trapped I am. Utterly helpless. All they have to do is coil some more of the plastic over my face and I won't be able to breath! Won't be able to scream!

Z asks me if I'm ok.

I say "yes".

Then I say, "I think I'm going to fall over".

I can hear the sound of the others sniffing their lines. Then feel the strong arms of the men round me, easing me down. My body is stiff, I am tilted and realise that I am being laid to rest on the futon. The falling seems to take an age. I feel that I am the Djed column of ancient Egypt and I am toppling...

Fig 5 – The Ritual of the Raising of the Djed pillar, from a contemporary papyrus.

The Djed is a pillar, a type of the World Tree, representing stability, continuity, and regeneration. The Festival of The Raising of the Djed dates back more than 5,000 years to predynastic times—as does the Egyptian Book of the Dead, which identifies the Djed as both the backbone of Osiris and the support and backbone of the universe. The Djed, however, is more than just an object; it is a mythic complex that existed long before Osiris emerged from the dark realm of the collective unconscious.

Historically, the Djed was raised at crucial transitional times between cycles, evoking light and stability to dispel darkness and disorder. Such periods were the Winter Solstices, the failing years of a reigning monarch or the coronation of a new one. However, according to the texts of the Temple of Horus at Edfu, the Djed served its greatest purpose and revealed its greatest mystery at the ending of one world age and the beginning of another. This is such a time!

From *The Raising of the Djed* by Moira Timms

I realise that I am outside my body. I can hear the woman outside somewhere talking. This is the guided visualisation. I am lying on a stone, inside a sarcophagus. I am inside a cube that reminds me of an iron pyrite crystal, greenish gold. The cube itself is inside a pyramid of bluish light. There is a night sky above me. The kind of sky you only get in the desert.

There seems to be silence. And out of the darkness peep millions of stars. I am under a blanket of stars or perhaps in a tent spangled with fireflies. The fabric of space glitters with all these jewels. I have forgotten that I've taken a drug. Forgotten that I'm taking part in a ritual. Forgotten my body and not even aware that I am wrapped up like a parcel. There is only the darkness and the twinkling lights. There is nothing before this. I have always been here. In the dark, in this space, nothing is before…

Then there is a desire to move. I begin to hear speech outside of my world (though with no conception that there is an 'outside'). Something about moving from earth to water, something about birth.

There it is again – that desire to move.

And yet I do not move, I have no idea that I can move. I have forgotten my body, my limbs, and my form.

Then I can feel something, it starts at my feet, as the words from outside get louder.

"…Ready to be re-born, to move and come into the light. From out of the earth into the waters of life…" There is music now, the rich tones of singing bowls, chanting and mantras. I feel my own chest resonate. I am intoning the mantra as well, a long, low Ommmmm, ahhhhhh, uhhhhhhh…

There it is at my ankles. Something is happening. A sound like a cutting, a slitting of fabric.

It seems so fast. The motion follows up my body. In an instant it reaches my penis. There is a moment of panic. There is a cold sensation on my skin. Is it water, is it fluid? Am I being born? Do I have a body or am I coming out of my cocoon as nothing more than a flood of liquid? Then I feel my legs. The ripping sensation moves up. I realise that the cold is from the bandage cutting scissors that are being used to open my wrapping. As the volume of the voices grows outside I feel myself joining in with the AUM mantra that is being sung, and moving. I can feel it now! I know that I have a definite form, a body of flesh and sinew and bone and lymph! I have four limbs and a rib cage! The binding is removed from my head. I have a head! A face, eyes, and I open them and smile.

They help me to sit and I look around. I have entered a space with these people where we are each an enlightened being. We have each crossed a spiritual abyss and now we sit together. Hands touching immersed in rapture. Each one of us is a vast Titan, like a series of giant statues of the Buddha. We sit together and sing the mantras of water. Into the ketamine space tumble words: "water, flow, keep it safe, keep it sacred, we are the water, share water, grok…"

If we want to change the world in a significant way, if we're serious about creating a better future for us all, then we have to face the fact that the only way it's going to happen is the only way it's ever happened: through the evolution of consciousness itself…We have to be the ones to create the future.

To accept responsibility for the future means we know without a doubt that it is on our own shoulders—each and every one of us—to create that future right now. We literally have to choose to be God—which I define as the creative or evolutionary impulse itself. Billions of years ago, something exploded out of nothing. And who but God could have made such an audacious choice—to create an entire universe? That powerful urge to become is now actually beginning to wake up, through the unique capacity for self-reflective awareness that is our human birthright. Through us, God, or the energy and intelligence that are driving this whole process, is just beginning to awaken to itself. So becoming God in an evolving universe means we have to be the ones to carry this process forward at the deepest and highest level, to consciously evolve in the biggest way possible for our collective salvation and transformation.

Spiritually, the enormous challenge for each and every one of us is to look directly into what it actually means to be the one who is going to do this. From the absolute or nondual perspective that emerges in spiritual revelation, there is only ONE. There literally is no other; there is only one without a second. To truly understand conscious evolution, we have to grapple with the profound implications of that absolute fact…That one without a second is simultaneously awakening to itself as it develops, as it evolves, and it is that one, as you and me, alone, that can now begin to take responsibility for endeavouring to consciously create its own future. That is enlightenment in an evolutionary context: the profound recognition that God is that singular energy and intelligence that initiated the creative process and is just now awakening to itself as we awaken to it. In that revelation, there literally is no other.

From *Divine Intervention* by Andrew Cohen

Then we take the water place it between us. The others have taken more ketamine and we are all at the same level. We place our hands on the glass and can feel it pulsing, moving with energy. Like a Ouija board it begins to rise up, great concentration (and yet a profound relaxation) is necessary to ensure that we don't drop this precious fluid. ("Keep it safe, keep it sacred".) The glass moves around, swinging in our hands around the circle. Our breath follows it as it settles into a circular motion.

"We are stirring the cauldron….

Turning the mill….

Water is the milk of the moon.

Share water…

(Keep it safe, keep it sacred…)

That all people might have water…

Clean and fresh…

The water of life…"

All these words, spoken to each person, weaving in and out, create a cycling invocation.

Then the water is placed on the ground.

One of the men offers me water.

"May you never thirst."

I drink and the water slips inside me (I have an inside!). I pass the magickal fluid to the man next to me.

"May you never thirst".

The water passes round the circle. As the last person drinks and replaces the cup on the table, the music stops.

Suddenly Yes! YES! YES! We are all shouting.

YES! I shout it again and everyone else joins in. Now we are kissing, the long passionate kisses of people who have just escaped death and found riches. People who find themselves possessed of the most delicious physical bodies, bodies that are relaxed, at ease and impossibly sensual.

YES! we all cry. Through mimicking death we have found new life. Yes is the sacred injunction of this Path. Saying 'yes' to life, to evolution, to discovery and even to death itself.

* * *

I wrote the account above soon after my initiation into what I think is one of the most interesting new belief systems of the early 21st century. The K-OS took me ages to track down. Little whispers on the Internet, a few intriguing hints from Austrian chaos magicians (a nation in which the cult seems particularly active). Very few people I have spoken to have heard of this approach to the sacramental use of ketamine, among the most potent of psychoactive drugs. The transmission itself comes drenched in a rich vocabulary of symbolism (though this vocabulary is far from fixed). However there are some elements of K-OS initiation iconography that neatly summarise much of the current's nature.

The triangle, as I have said, is a key symbol in the cult and the gateway to the K-OS initiation process. One of the symbolic tools used in the cult is a pyramid (often of crystal or glass) used to crush the ketamine into a fine powder if it is to be insufflated. On emerging into the ketamine space (after being unwrapped) I was deeply aware of the fact that each member of the group (sitting with legs crossed in a circle) was an illuminated adept, that is a magician active in the sephira of Binah.

Within the mystical system of Thelema, The City of the Pyramids is the home to those adepts that have crossed the great Abyss, having spilled all their blood in the Graal of Babalon. They have destroyed their earthly ego-identities, becoming nothing more than piles of dust (i.e. the remaining aspects of their True Selves without the self-sense of "I"), and become impregnated as a Babe within Babalon. Within, they take on the name or title of Saint or Nemo (Latin for No-Man). In the system of A.'.A.'. they are called Masters of the Temple. It is a step along the path of spiritual purification, and a resting place for those who have successfully shed their attachments to the mundane world.

Of these adepts, it is written in Aleister Crowley's *The Vision and The Voice* (Aethyr 14):

"These adepts seem like Pyramids—their hoods and robes are like Pyramids.

And the Angel sayeth: Verily is the Pyramid a Temple of Initiation. Verily also is it a tomb…"

And from Wikipedia,
The City exists under the Night of Pan (or N.O.X.) within the sephira of Binah on the Tree of Life. [The Night of Pan is] …a mystical state that represents the stage of ego-death in the process of spiritual attainment…Pan is both the giver and the taker of life, and his Night is that time of symbolic death where the adept experiences unification with the All through the ecstatic destruction of the ego-self. In a more general sense, it is the state where one transcends all limitations and experiences oneness with the universe.

Ketamine is a drug I'd used before but one for which there is no traditional use. However it seemed to sit perfectly here, as an ally in crossing the Abyss. The mythology of the K-OS itself teaches that the magickal use of ketamine was initially transmitted to John C. Lilly during his experiments with this substance.

As Lilly floated in the isolation tank fluid, Enright injected him with 35 milligrams of Ketamine (K). Within a few minutes, Lilly could actually visualize the migraine pain moving out of his skull, to a point levitated there in apperceived space, Lilly felt no pain whatsoever for some twenty minutes, until it once again re-entered his head. When Lilly began moaning and groaning in his water-filled sanctum of pain, Enright injected him with another 70 milligrams. This time Lilly felt the pain moving farther away, twelve feet this time. Thirty minutes later the migraine lightning bolt of pain came rushing back, lodging itself once again into Dr. Lilly's head. Enright reloaded his syringe and shot the good doctor up with 150 milligrams. This time when the pain vacated Lilly's head it kept on going and didn't come back; clear over the horizon, never to be seen again. An hour later, after the K wore off, Lilly climbed out of the tank, a new man...

...further solo flights on K...reaffirmed his deeply held conviction that his life was being watched over by higher powers of an extra-terrestrial origin.

John Lilly, Ketamine and The Entities From ECCO - by Adam Gorightly (exclusive to ConspiracyArchive.com)

Lilly famously experimented with taking ketamine in various sensory deprivation environments and even when diving with dolphins. And it is the dolphins that form one of the most curious elements of the K-OS mythology. They believe (or at least claim they believe) that their tradition was transmitted through Lilly from the dolphins he interacted with when he was the director of the Communications Research Institute at St. Thomas in the Virgin Islands. Here Lilly spent years exploring the possibilities of inter-species communication. "The dolphins transmitted the system to Lilly" one initiate told me "the dolphins had downloaded their wisdom from the ancient sunken library of the Atlantians. They gave the instructions for initiation to Lilly when he was swimming with them. That's where many of his revelations really came from". (Lilly recounts many of his insights in his 'metaphysical autobiography *The Scientist*. As the book's blurb explains the texts concerns "…communication with extra-terrestrials and the imperative of dolphin/human dialog.") Naturally the Atlantian library is imagined as a huge sunken pyramid.

> "Even the nose is a triangle, a pyramid, and it's from that first breath, through our noses, that we come alive". And this is the central process of the K-OS, dying in order to feel more fully alive, entering the tomb and undoing all our habitual body armour from the most literal physical level in order to achieve transformation".
>
> A Brother of K-OS

So what does the dolphin gnosis tell us? What is the central message "It's all about love" another initiate told me. "The leader of the dolphins tells us that they just want to bring us water and tell us to love ourselves and each other. Just get them (humans) to be nice to each other."

Jokingly I asked if the leader of the dolphins was called Howard (after the talking dolphin in Illuminatus!). "No", I was told, "the transmission tells us that the Atlantian dolphin God is called 'snorky'".

Fig 6 – Cover artwork of Illuminatus!

The Pope & The Prophet

"I admit that my visions can never mean to other men as much as they do to me. I do not regret this. All I ask is that my results should convince seekers after truth that there is beyond doubt something worthwhile seeking, attainable by methods more or less like mine. I do not want to father a flock, to be the fetish of fools and fanatics, or the founder of a faith whose followers are content to echo my opinions. I want each man to cut his own way through the jungle." Aleister Crowley

"An Enlightened Master is ideal only if your goal is to become a Benighted Slave." Robert Anton Wilson

From the brilliant introduction to why it's worth exploring meditation in *Book 4*, through to the poetic genius of *The Book of the Law*, Crowley is an excellent writer. He dives deep into metaphysical speculation, Qabalistic exegesis, grand political pronouncements and rakish humour. But like the brilliant Robert Anton Wilson he also says over and over again that the map is not the territory.

Sadly the triumph of style over content (and let's face it with Crowley there is one hell of a lot of style as well as content) means that it's remarkably easy to adore the sparkling wrapper and miss the challenging gift you've found inside.

I've had some lovely conversations with Thelemites recently and, don't get me wrong, I enjoy doing line by line analysis of *Liber AL* as much as the next occult-trainspotter geek, BUT…

Why does it have to happen again and again that a teacher arrives, proclaims that we should all 'think for ourselves and question authority', and yet ends up being the centre of a personality cult? That's why I find that 'proclaiming the Law of Thelema' thing tricky. Sure I'm down with it that Thelema is an expression of a perennial philosophy, which arises in Buddhism, Taoism, Tantrism, and indeed the esoteric traditions of many faiths. Not that Crowley himself didn't, at times, write clear injunctions for his followers to spread his word and his cult as The

Prophet of The New Aeon. Frankly I've been remiss on not writing that at some point myself so, for the record; please send me your money, offers of assistance etc so that I can set up a Brave New World of Pleasure and Freedom and Power with me as Supreme Czar and my book *Magick Works* as the core sacred text. Thank you.

The Law – definite article. Hang on? We've been here before haven't we? The Law of Moses, The Holy Bible – thousands of years and lifetimes of madness later and Crowley, the great trickster, the demon Crowley, tries the trick again and – oh dear...

So to reference dear Ol' Ramsey Dukes again I'd say that I 'dig' Thelema. No I'm not going to photocopy and distribute copies of *Liber Oz* round my old university campus, but I do dig it.

So I guess I'm a Thelemite in the same sense that I'm a Wiccan, a Pagan, and many other things. It's part of my personal magickal blend but I wouldn't want it to overwhelm all the other rich flavours. Crowley's teacher Alan Bennett was one of the first people to introduce Buddhism to the West, and Crowley himself studied long and hard in the East. *The Book of The Law* is so clearly a Sufi text that it's hardly worth much more comment. Sure it's got some fabulous stuff in it, and some derivative rambling, some maniac coke-head ravings and a couple of bonkers embedded Sudoku puzzles... But I can't (as I believe one must to become an initiate of the OTO) accept *The Book of The Law* as THE word of God (I suspect that's not the exact wording but my Minerval was some time ago). Now please appreciate I'm not saying Thelemites are stupid, that they've never considered these things. I'm sure many have. It just seems to me that by focusing on his religion of Thelema we miss out on so much more of what Crowley was about. It leaves us emulating how he produced his books, his liberal use of Greek letters, his fetish for insignia and ceremonial titles. But this isn't Crowley the magician and teacher. He comes over so well in texts like *The Book of Thoth* in which, while steadfast in its Thelema, uses this as a steady burning torch that leads us towards discovery. The torch is to guide us through the darkness and into the light of a New Aeon, not for us to sit down around and worship.

Crowley always wanted to be a preacher, like his Dad who died of tongue cancer (I mean how darkly poetic can you get?) when 'Alick' was still young and whom he described as his 'hero'. So of course he fancied himself as head of a religion. It doesn't take a brilliant psychologist to see why. But he also engaged in systematic and determined magick to transform himself. He carried magick out of the medieval grimoire tradition and into the modern age. What a staggering achievement! Creating his own religion is a footnote compared to that Herculean effort. That's why the introduction to *Book 4* rules. And that's why, especially as a magician, my tribute to Crowley is to be me.

They Rise

The true purpose of humanity is revealed.

"Thing is you've heard all the stories, all those weird tales. You've read the books, seen the YouTube videos, maybe cultists have even contacted you! Man, shit! I probably shouldn't be talking to you."

My contact was paranoid. Much as I'd expected. After all, in this game, you really had to be paranoid. Paranoid or mad, that was the choice.

He was a small nervous man; slightly camp, dressed in standard issue black Mac though lacking any of the usual ominous bling that I'd come to expect. On the surface he wasn't much different to the others I'd met. Neurotic, hasty, apt to glance around him as though 'they' were undoubtedly closing in. But what made this guy different was not just the angle he took on the conspiracy. It was also what he did for a living. Sure all kinds of people claimed all kinds of 'special access' to the real truth. But for this guy the story checked out. He was certainly there when it happened.

"The Elder Gods, the deep ones, the entities from between the spaces. You know…" he glanced once more conspiratorially around. "It's true. From the spaces between the stars, they are coming back and there's nothing we can do to stop them.

I've seen it. In Antarctica, at the research station. We were drilling, prospecting. This was about five years ago. The cover was that we were taking core samples. Checking the ice for data about climate change. Fuckin' joke!"

"Joke?"

"Well the climate thing, that's part of their plan. It's part of the inheritance they've left us with. A seed, a homing device. We're opening the gate for their return, all of us, ever since the industrial revolution.

Look let me get this straight. You believe me don't you?"

"Yes, yes I do."

"Well it's not about monsters, at least not in the way you probably think. Lovecraft was on to it, then those guys from the Miskatonic Alchemical Expedition. But most of them, the researchers, the cultists, they have no idea, no fucking idea at all."

I nodded for him to continue.

"So I'm part of the drilling team. We're going deep, after the big prize, access to the world's last great untapped oil reserves. We know they are there. In the rock above there are loads of salt deposits. These generally sit above the oil, capping it, keeping it in position. Like a circle of salt trapping a slug.

We're drilling down, almost at the reservoir. We're expecting the oil to start coming up pretty fast. We're talking huge pressures here. Rock and half a kilometre of ice as well bearing down on this huge pustule of oil."

He drank. Was silent for a moment. Then blurted it out.

"We saw them man. There they were in the darkness. We had ultrasound imagining on the drilling rig. Well a huge collection of instruments really. Infrared detectors, seismic monitors, all kinds of stuff. Ours was going to be the first hole down there and we needed to gather data. The rest of the operation, bringing out the big rigs to drill, we needed to tell them the geology. We knew that the environmentalists would go ape shit when they found out what was going on. So we wanted a done deal. Besides people are starving! What the fuck are we doing? It takes so much fossil fuel to make even a fucking lettuce! We can't even feed ourselves without oil!"

I let him rant until he'd got it out of his system. I opened a pack of crisps and offered him some. Distracted, he was knocked back on track, back to the story I so wanted to hear.

"What we saw was unlike anything I've ever seen. We detected them first in the ultra-violet spectrum. Shapes. We thought at first they had to be geological features. Some kind of huge volcanic structures. There were maybe seven or eight we could see clearly, though the other instruments suggested there could be as many as twenty-three."

I raised an eyebrow at the mention of the magick number. This was a mistake. He pulled back from the table, hissed in a breath.

"Look if you think this is all bullshit it's over man. I'm exposing myself enough just meeting you here. You may think I'm batshit crazy, but, well, fuck…"

Holding out my hands in a supplicatory gesture I said,

"No, I don't think it's bullshit. Please carry on." He eyed me for a moment and then resumed his monologue.

"So they are moving, these 'volcanoes', like they are dancing or something. The instruments in the drilling system are detecting movement. We plot the data on the computers and this picture starts to build up. A whole bunch of conical structures, some as large as a hundred feet tall. One has a projection coming from the apex of the triangle. A long," - he hesitated, "A long fucking neck man, a neck with one huge eye on the end!"

I nodded; this was what I'd already heard. I tried to look surprised but not incredulous.

"So what happened?"

"Well man we just didn't know what it was all about! There was an argument; the project manager accused the IT guys of taking the piss. Setting up some kind of spooky images in the data. He checked everything, ordered the rest of us around like we were in some fucking military unit. It was like he was trying to hold onto what was going on and instead he just lost it."

"Did he commit suicide that day?" I asked.

"As far as we can tell. Apparently when it all came out the medic with us said he'd already been on anti-depressants. Not sleeping either. Not that we didn't know that, our quarters were in the same pod, for weeks I'd been woken by him, sobbing or crying. First time I heard him cry out in the night I thought I was hearing an animal. Course there's nothing alive out there, in Antarctica, so I quickly realised it was one of us. Sounded like an animal in a trap, injured or something.

Yeah so the manager just switches off all the imagining systems. He says something about them being fucked, ghost images, errors in the data. He told us to keep drilling and get ready to take samples direct of the oil. Then he left."

"He went outside?"

"As far as we can tell. He just left the room, walked down the corridor towards the main door. Let himself out and walked off."

"How low was the outside temperature?" I asked.

My contact shuddered involuntarily and hunched over.

"Man it must have been about minus 30 at least. I hated it, all the cold, and those huge plains of ice. Cold so deep that it could freeze off your fingers in seconds if they were exposed. Freeze your piss before it hits the ground."

He returned to his ranting mode.

"Man that's why we don't live there, humans I mean. The one landmass that we stayed away from. That cold isn't the cold of the earth. It's the cold of space. It's alien, know what I mean?"

I nodded, "another drink?"

"No. I gotta go soon. See my doctor; get something to calm me down."

He mimed a snorting motion, must be scoring ketamine to get through I guessed.

"So what happened, after you breached the chamber, you started to get the oil?"

"Well man it just came up, you know, gushing black. Real rushes, so we got the cap on and the pipes into position. I didn't see much of that because my job was all the instrumentation. I switched the detection systems back on. Nothing, no weird volcanoes, no mysterious towers with eyes. Nothing. Just the radiant ultra-violet colours of some of the finest quality oil this planet still has to offer. It was like we'd all had this mental dream. Some people doubted what they'd seen, especially after I ran back through the data and couldn't see anything. The logs were just full of glitches; most of the files wouldn't load. We were left depending on our diminishing memories. Anyhow it wasn't until a couple of hours later that we discovered the Boss had taken a walk. A team went outside and looked for his body. Conditions were perfect, bright midnight sun, and they found him in less than 20 minutes. Poor bastard had taken all his clothes off and it looked like he'd cut himself on the chest."

"The Elder sign?" It seemed an obvious bet.

"Yes. Not that I knew it at the time. Not till much later. I was only out there for another couple of weeks. Nothing went wrong after that. The company arranged for this new guy to be flown in. Norwegian, solid as a rock, only cared about the production and kept himself to himself. I flew out five days after he arrived for some R&R. Came back here to Britain, fucking lucky, or something."

"So after you left, that's when the other deaths happened?"

"Yeah. No one knows the details, or if they do they sure didn't release them to us. Some of those people were my friends."

He sat silent for a moment, collected himself, and ran his hands across his face.

"All we really know is that all twenty members of the crew, from the cook to the captain died. There were no signs of a struggle; it was like they all decided to leave the station one day. Their bodies were all found, naked, scattered like chunks of frozen meat around the buildings. They'd all gone outside, gone mad, whatever, they were all dead.

They flew the bodies back. I went to three of the funerals. Confused looking parents crying, trying to make sense of the senseless. I didn't go to any more. Too depressing and I'd already started to realise I was being watched."

"By whom?"

"Man, I don't fucking know! The Illuminati, the police, MI5, CIA, could be anyone! I leave my flat and there, on the other side of the street, is this big car. Two guys inside watching the house. Then, three days later, I went to Scotland to see my mum. I noticed this spooky black van, followed me all the fucking way! What's that all about?

But it's the dreams, which are the worst. Once I came back they started. I tried to hold them off, tried to drink or smoke myself stupid every night. But now I do K and try to blot it out, or maybe just accept it. Fact is that I'm on my way out. Cancer. It's got me, so I've got nothing to lose. That's why I'm here. That's why I'm telling you this. You've gotta know the truth."

"Tell me!" I thought. I leant forward. This could be it. Really. The revelation. The final piece of the puzzle.

"It's the oil, man. The Old Ones from ancient times when the earth was new. They're in the oil! Our species is addicted to it. We need it, for food, industry, and medicine. We're summoning them, again and again, through huge drilling machines spewing eternal flames. They're coming back all right and we're doing it for them! Filling the air with carbon, warming the world. Bringing it back to the way it was in the Carboniferous when they ruled. Soon the earth will be nothing but a vast, warm swamp. Giant insects roaming the land. Steamy forests of horsetails.

All of us monkeys, were just going to get cancer and die, that's if the famine and flash floods don't finish us first. Hydrocarbon toxicity is going up and up. That stuff from Antarctica, that's going to finish it. We're like that thing, Shub-Niggurath, the Goat of a Thousand Young. We've bred billions of ourselves, fouling our own nest like a sickness. As the world warms up, thunk! There's another baby, thunk, thunk, thunk! Another million babies, crying and yelling! The Old Ones are coming back and there's nothing we can do. It's like the cancer inside me right now, eating me up from the inside. Oil - it's the blood of the Elder race."

"So what now?" I asked. "If that's the truth, if this drilling in Antarctica is the last straw, what can we do?"

"Do, do? Nothing! Well go ahead buy tinned food and guns if it makes you happier. When we finally fall upon each other like wild beasts it won't make much difference. We've passed the tipping point. Soon, and believe me it'll be soon, they're going to reveal themselves. Like those things I saw in that oil field. They'll be walking on the earth, as the weather goes insane and the temperatures rise. In a hundred years' time it's just going to be the insects, the jellyfish and them. They're coming back and we've summoned them! With every nodding donkey, with each oilrig, each bright carbon flare. There's no-where to hide, not even in your own mind!"

He stood, glanced around and made to go. Before he left he bend down and whispered:

"Don't bother trying to contact me again. I'm leaving this time for good. Going to take me a nice warm bath and some ketty heaven. I'm getting off this stage right now, before the whole shit house goes up in flames."

Conversation in the pub carried on around me after he left. But I wasn't seeing the people anymore. Just puppets dancing, the playthings of the black carbon Gods from deep within the earth. I knew what I'd heard was true, they were rising just like the sea level, and there was nothing I or anyone else could do.

Of course it all made sense. It certainly chimed in with what I'd already discovered about the jellyfish. You've not heard? Well it goes like this. Jellyfish are amazing, weird animals. They've existed on our earth for at least 500 millions of years. They look like any other weird animal floating round in the oceans, but they are really special. A jellyfish is a community organism. That means that they are made up of millions of autonomous cells that choose to conglomerate together. It's the original hive mind, a biological conspiracy. And what's more they are clever, and they know how to play the long game.

Jellyfish of course live in the ocean. And it's into that same ocean that our species has been pouring fertility. Vast amounts of ammonium nitrate and other fertilisers get washed into it every year. By burning all those fossil fuels and doing slash and burn agriculture we've kept the planet's temperature nice and warm. Rather than being headed toward another ice age, which would be expected given the cycles in the geological record, the planet is snug. The sea is warming up too and getting more acidic. This is another one of the reasons that we're seeing jellyfish in huge numbers. They turn up off the coast of Japan in tens of thousands, some as big as refrigerators. The formerly 'exotic' and poisonous Portuguese man-of-war is now to be found bobbing around the British Isles. The number of other species in our waters has gone up tremendously, as has their size. You'll find jellyfish the size of tractor tyres regularly washed ashore on the Welsh coast.

But it's not just their size and their numbers. It's what they can eat.

In the oceans of our planet there are now gigantic rafts of plastic. These are swept by the ocean currents into huge gyring mats that, amongst other things, are white and serve to heat the planet up even more. They reflect the light back into the atmosphere, warming it still further. These rafts are so huge you can see them on Google Earth, try it for yourself.

Now of course lots of animals get injured or poisoned by the plastics. Seals get garrotted; tiny fish fill their bellies with plastic debris and cannot feed. Turtles eat plastic bags and choke, thinking that they are jellyfish.

But jellyfish are one of the only animals that can metabolise plastic. They can absorb it into their bodies and lock it away safely in their cells. It may even be one of the things that are allowing them to grow larger. The jellyfish take up the plasticized molecules and actually use them to strengthen their cell membranes. This means larger, more complex shapes of jellyfish are turning up.

Nature normally keeps jellyfish numbers in check by predating fish. But we humans have killed most of the top carnivores in the sea. We're eaten all the fish that would usually be munching through the jellyfish. So that, plus all the fertiliser, and the jellyfish population explodes.

So the deal is this. Humans only purpose is to invoke the Great Old Ones, the darkness of millions of year's old oil. We burn this; we manufacture plastics, fish the seas empty and then cook up a warm nutrient rich soup for the jellyfish to breed in.

The jellyfish are the Elder Gods reborn. As they thrive in the world that we have created, a world in which we are doomed, they rise. They will absorb the plastic that is literally everywhere on the earth and build new bodies. They will migrate from the seas onto a land devoid of many of the mammalian and other species. Safe in this evolutionary downtime they will grow into who knows what wonderful and monstrous forms? Perhaps it is they who will go to the stars. It's the jellyfish that will take the living seeds of Gaia into space. And maybe that's been her plan all along? Gaia, evolving us, a clever ape that knows how to dig and to make fire. We're just here to generate the plastics. To avert the ice age and instead create just the right conditions for the really important actors in the drama to squelch forward. The jellyfish, perhaps as few as thousands of years from now, could be the dominant intelligent species on the planet. They could be the ones reaching for the stars.

Insane? Perhaps. But consider this. Consider the mythology of the Old Ones. Not just the Lovecraftian fantasy but also the nameless horror in the deep of earth and space, the horror that you know exists. Imagine these forms, plastic jellyfish entities, migrating from the warm ocean onto the post-apocalyptic world. Well apocalyptic for us, for our species, and countless others. But for them this will be their moment of glory. They are the supreme intelligence that's really running things. And you surely can't deny that you've always thought that a) something is behind all of this and b) that the mind that is really in control of reality is something inscrutably alien.

The signs are all around. That eye in the triangle. It's a fucking sentient jellyfish, taking off into space! We're just the booster rocket of their species. We are Gaia's way of metabolising plastic, of using all that locked up carbon. That ancient darkness liberated by us insane monkeys, all to send her pulsating viscid children into space.

Look at the UFO. It's a jellyfish!

Still sceptical? Then check this out;

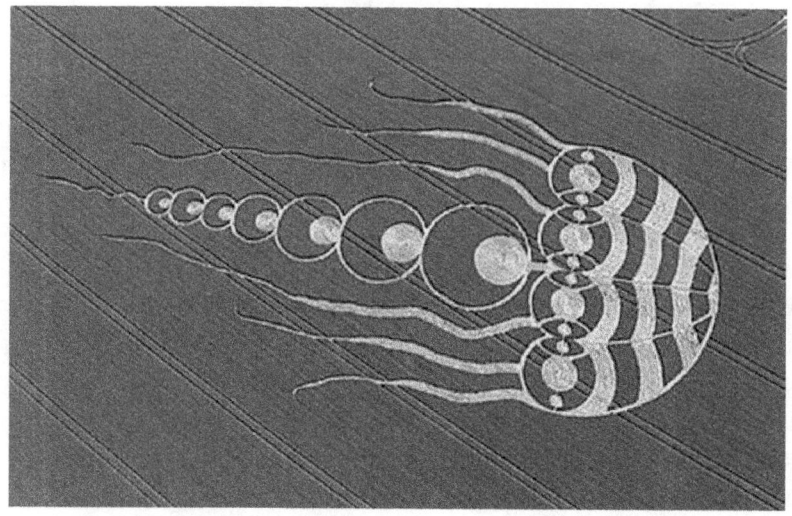

Fig 7 – I for one welcome our jellyfish overlords.

Giant jellyfish invades Earth… in the form of a mysterious crop circle

By *DAILY MAIL* REPORTER

Last updated at 8:52 PM on 02nd June 2009

No one had ever seen a jellyfish like this before – particularly not in the middle of a farmer's field.

The 600ft monster, similar to a giant Portuguese man-of-war, has delighted crop circle watchers by turning up near Kingstone Coombes, Oxfordshire.

And listen to what the article says:

Crop circle expert Karen Alexander said: 'We have seen butterfly and bird patterns in the past, but this is the first jellyfish crop circle in the world. It is absolutely huge; three times the size of most patterns,

and extremely interesting. People have been aghast at the size of it. It is a complete monster.

We are looking into the meaning of it, but at present it just seems to have appeared out of nowhere.'

A monster appearing out of nowhere? Really? No, we should all have seen this coming, though many of us have felt this even before we understood the real horror.

You look like an intelligent person. You've had your suspicions I'm sure, and now you can see how it all connects. Every last tentacle.

Now do you believe?

Beyond the Pharmakon

> "It's funny how people think the Bible is from God, when it's obviously just another book written by people!"
> Osric Gray

When the ibis headed God Thoth first proposed writing I'm sure he realised what a joke he was having at the expense of humanity. Writing is the Pharmakon, a bane and blessing all in one handy set of marks on a page. This is the story of how a secret wisdom has begun to emerge in the world that has been kept hidden precisely because of our orientation, especially in the Western world, towards that which is written.

Writing happens around the dawn of agriculture. Unevenly spread around the globe, systems of signs had existed before writing, as we know it, for millennia. There are three regions of our planet where Thoth's gift appears. The Middle East in the fabled Fertile Crescent and caressing the banks of the river Nile. In his form of supreme deity, sorcerer and shaman Itzamna provides the Maya with literacy. And in China, as the ancient sage Ts'ang Chieh, he introduces sacred marks onto oracle bones. Writing grew up with our first truly domesticated grains (wheat, corn, rice in each of the three regions). Time begins; calendrical systems of great stellar inspired complexity are set in motion. Elaborate mathematics, that phemonologically austere form of writing, develops as pyramids and ziggurats and palaces arise.

Writing is magick, it creates a new world for those who can understand it, the literasphere, part of the record of the noosphere. Without it government is impossible, after all taxes need to be collected and this necessitates record keeping. Writing begins to refer back to itself; it creates what we call history. Writing carries ideas; the names of Gods and the special marks that it comprises are venerated, sacred glyphs. Hebrew script, Sanskrit letters, Chinese characters. Words are so powerful in ancient Egypt that snake bites can be charged away by simply pressing the names of Isis written on strip of papyrus to the wound. In South America Mayan hieroglyphs are carved into gigantic temples causing them to remain standing until the end of time. Kings set up stelae and shrine posts and propaganda is born.

"Nebuchadnezzar, King of Babylon, the faithful prince appointed by the will of Marduk, the highest of princely princes, beloved of Nabu, of prudent counsel, who has learned to embrace wisdom, who fathomed their divine being and reveres their majesty, the untiring governor, who always takes to heart the care of the cult of Esagila and Ezida and is constantly concerned with the well-being of Babylon and Borsippa, the wise, the humble, the caretaker of Esagila and Ezida, the firstborn son of Nabopolassar, the King of Babylon.

Both gate entrances of Imgur-Ellil and Nemetti-Ellil —following the filling of the street from Babylon—had become increasingly lower. Therefore, I pulled down these gates and laid their foundations at the water table with asphalt and bricks and had them made of bricks with blue stone on which wonderful bulls and dragons were depicted. I covered their roofs by laying majestic cedars length-wise over them. I hung doors of cedar adorned with bronze at all the gate openings. I placed wild bulls and ferocious dragons in the gateways and thus adorned them with luxurious splendour so that people might gaze on them in wonder.

I let the temple of Esiskursiskur (the highest festival house of Marduk, the Lord of the Gods—a place of joy and celebration for the major and minor Gods) be built firm like a mountain in the precinct of Babylon of asphalt and fired bricks."

Such is the inscription emblazoned on the monstrously tall Ishtar gate of Babylon (It is unlikely that the use of the first person pronoun in this dedication should be taken to suggest our King was a DIY guru.)

Writing always points to more writing. The skill in those who learn to read becomes effortless. So natural, perhaps indicating that writing slept, unnoticed in the mind of every human since the dawn of time. But when that switch is flicked, words jump out and they cannot help but be read.

Pretty much from day one, the Gods themselves are showing literary pretensions. The deities actually write. From such sacred texts the author disappears (way before the post-modernists would have us believe) and the text is itself divine. Deity creates scripture and creates history, all we can do is memorise or read or comment on this holy writ.

Cut to a few hundreds of years later. Moses has had those tablets, Buddha has penned his sutras as the embodiment of enlightenment, and Mohammed gets the Koran (that our logo maniacal monotheist author chooses to release as cut-up text over a period of some two decades). The plurality of the Classical period writing becomes submerged in the literature of a singular divine provenance. In the style of Terry Pratchett's one might imagine the basic argument; "Look mate, it's the word of God not some bunch of bow-backed sissy scribes. It's not people wot wrote this stuff it's from Him upstairs!"

And so we arrive at the dawn of literalism. Christianity, which is basically the Jewish take on the Classical mystery cults of Seraphis and Mithras, splits into two camps. There are the Gnostics, they hold that Christianity is a religion of experience, a series of initiations of which only the outer court mystery doctrine asserts that Jesus was an historical figure. Then there are those who claim that Biblical texts are literally the Word of God. When God says he made the world in six days that's exactly what he means. The fact that Pagan theologians of the time took the piss out of a supreme being who sounded more like a navvy was neither here nor there. Jesus was an actual man; indeed his nativity becomes the benchmark of history itself, BC/AD. Meanwhile literalist Islam has to put up with its own interpretation-happy gnosticated mystics the Sufis. They argue for a direct personal revelation through practices such as whirling dances, prayer, music and sometimes drinking, partying and laughing.

So the literalist rulers (who incidentally make sure that the literal word of God remains inaccessible to the great unwashed by jealously guarding literacy) come down hard on these Gnostic voices. The cacophony of multiple interpretations must be silenced. There is only one interpretation of the revealed word of God. Heresy is invented and torturers find that business is booming. As monotheism rises like a tower from the chaotic mass of polytheism multiple interpretations of writing are silenced. The *Gospel of Thomas* is thrown out. Lost in the desert along with the *Thunder of a Perfect Mind*.

So these heretical groups, those deviant ideologies, go underground. The history of the Knights Templars is one example of this process. Whatever the truth of their alleged crimes after the first decades of the 14th century they vanish from political history, apparently comprehensively smashed up thanks to Philip the Fair of France. Baphomet, buggery and blasphemy churn together in the political ferment of the time. Along with the allegation that the Templars are taking each other's confessions; the Brothers, it would seem, are doing it for themselves. Not to mention of course all that consorting with the Old Man of the Mountains, he of 'Nothing is True, Everything is Permitted' fame. Such relations, especially when allied to such a brilliant financial acumen, will undoubtedly breed suspicion.

And the secret brotherhood of the Templars goes literally underground

Perhaps decades after their Order has been crushed the heirs to the Templar mysteries end up in a cave in Royston, Hertfordshire fifty miles north of London. Today the cave is accessed down a long tunnel that descends gradually, sloping towards the foot of the chamber. The cave itself is an artificial structure cut from the chalk that underlies this area. Its shape is vaguely conical, only a few meters wide at the base and tapering to a point towards the surface. High above the floor of the cave one can see the original entrance. This hole was cunningly hidden, as was the chimney, which was vented through the hearth of the building that used to stand above the chamber. When the place was first carved out, sometime in the 14th century, visitors would have had to crawl through a small opening at the roof. They would have alighted onto a wooden platform shaped like a hexagram. To one side of the platform was a huge cresset on a movable arm. Pose-able mood lighting for whatever went on there perhaps? A trap door through the platform permitted access, via a ladder, to the base of the cave. Here an octagonal floor was created. Pillars holding the hexagram platform up were struck down into this eight-sided figure, their measurements and number recalls exactly the architecture of the Dome of the Rock. On one side of the lower chamber there is a scoop of earth, foetus shaped but man sized, known as 'the grave'. All around the lower chamber are carvings. There are doves and knights and a scene of a man being burned at the stake. There are abstract designs and symbols that, before the structure was abandoned, seem to have been deliberately excised. When the site was re-discovered in the 18th century it was found that the cave had been filled in with soft topsoil. Whoever did the work wanted to hide, but not destroy this mysterious cell.

In a prominent position in the cave is a carving of Saint Catherine, a patron of Templars. This, along with what appears to be the scene showing Jacques de Molay being executed, suggests that whoever was using this cave was at least inspired by, if not the direct cultural descendants of, the Templars. Why Saint Catherine? Perhaps because she is the Christian counterpart to the Pagan Hypatia, the brilliant and martyred scholar of Alexandria. The archetypal Wise Woman.

Who used this place? Hidden beneath the earth, at the exact intersection of two ancient Roman roads? Whatever they were up to was certainly a dangerous business. This was undoubtedly a nest for heretics. But the building that existed above the site would have afforded some protection. It was occasionally used as a hunting lodge. A place where men from many different backgrounds could meet and stay the night without arousing suspicion. From their lodge our guests would have descended into the subterranean space, and perhaps into an initiated tradition.

Look amongst the carvings and you can see the symbols of early Freemasonry, the Brothers who also meet in the lodge.

So what might the secret of the Templars be, some Gnostic heresy perhaps? Some ancient mystery cult? The tiny seed of the International Banking and Illuminati conspiracy for a New World Order and One World Government?

The story of the Templars is obscure but we do know about their spiritual descendants, the Freemasons and those practitioners of the occult arts that we call magicians.

Cut to the late 1500s. Dr John Dee and Edward Kelly draw their circle to conjure the shade of a dead man. In doing so they stand in deeply practical terms in the same tradition as the Gnostics. Through direct experience, through experiment, they are seeking to understand the universe. They create a special place, a laboratory if you will, where by knowing the secret laws of the universe, they can cause miraculous effects.

This is magick, this is Gnosticism, the direct experimental approach to reality. The suggestion that if we wish to know the mind of God we should do so through experience not second hand through holy writ alone.

There is a pointer to a deep process in the structure of the magick circle.

The magician stands in the circle. The circle defines the universe and here he is God. He defines the initial conditions of the space and performs operations in that space according to a blend of inspiration and ceremonial formula. In this space he gains knowledge, discovers treasure.

The scientist stands in her laboratory. The laboratory defines the universe and here she is God. She defines the initial conditions of the space and performs operations in that space according to a blend of inspiration and accepted formula. In this space she gains knowledge, discovers treasure.

Of course some people don't dig this approach to God (and indeed in the second millennium of the Christian era one could easily get into plenty of trouble with the authorities for pursuing such magical experiments). The guardians of the Status Quo preferred instead the apparent certainty offered by the divine as revealed through literal and conventionally interpreted Holy text. And there is no appeal to common human experience, what we might call the 'real world' that is acceptable. Galileo (who is around just a little after Dee dies) might well claim there are moons to be seen orbiting Jupiter. But we may simply refuse to peer through his telescope, convinced in our *a priori* certainty that they are illusory. The pious guardians of Church doctrine refuse to have any truck with such devilish devices as telescopes, microscopes and other heretical ways of seeing.

So mindful of Galileo's house arrest the Gnostic search for the divine continues through the centuries. It secretly fulminates in a network of intellectuals known as The Invisible College.

Wikipedia teaches us that:
"The idea of an invisible college became influential in seventeenth

century Europe, in particular, in the form of a network of savants or intellectuals exchanging ideas (by post, as it would have been understood at the time). This is an alternative model to that of the learned journal, dominant in the nineteenth century. The invisible college idea is exemplified by the network of astronomers, professors, mathematicians, and natural philosophers in 16th century Europe. Men such as Johannes Kepler, Georg Joachim Rheticus, John Dee and Tycho Brahe passed information and ideas to each other in an invisible college. One of the most common methods used to communicate was through marginalia, annotations written in personal copies of books that were loaned, given, or sold."

An early attempt at creating discussion threads via a hard copy implementation of the Internet?

Such clandestine networks and organised societies, of which the Templars and their spiritual sons the Masons were the ancient template, are perhaps really in possession of a marvellous secret. A Philosophers Stone that is not a literal substance but an idea, which was (in the early modern period) about to ignite the world. This idea is the notion that God is to be found through experiment in the world of nature. That experiment can legitimately extend into any dimension; theological, social, military, medical and in the case of John Dee and the wife swapping Edward Kelly, sexual. In this emerging universe the only authority is experiential and there is a growing recognition that Church and Crown have hoodwinked humanity into bowing before an empty throne. God may not be dead (yet) but if we are to know Him then the Gnostic process is the only game in town. Masonic groups of the period were creating temporal autonomous zones where men of different social spheres could meet in an ecumenical secrecy and discuss ideas. Networks such as the Rosicrucians and Invisible College were distributing these ideas across national borders.

Then in 1660 the Invisible College goes public, backed this time by the King who is anxious to secure maritime supremacy for Britain. The aim is to use the boffins to come up with better navigational techniques and weapons. By permitting this space to exist after the carnage of the English Civil War the King and his viziers aim to rebuild the flagging international fortunes of the country. They make the connections, bringing the Invisible Alumni in from the cold. 'the Royal Society of London for the Improvement of Natural Knowledge' is born. The motto of The Royal Society was, and remains to this day "nullius in verba", which may be translated as "Take nobody's word for it" or, as four hundred or so years later as a scientist from the colonies would put it, "think for yourself and question authority".

And so begins the history of the discourse that we know as science.

These days, or perhaps more accurately a few decades ago, this rise in scientific practice might have been described as the slow triumph of the rational mind over superstition, religion and occultism. However today we know that's far from the whole story. Indeed as chemistry is born from alchemy, so too many of the heroes of science have been pursuing these studies from a clearly gnostic perspective. That is they are investigating the world not simply to know how it works (to make bigger and better battleships for the King) but because by doing so they are coming to know the Mind of God. Just a few examples; Joseph Priestly, who first isolated the gas that later was named oxygen, was a Dissenting Minister clergyman for whom science would usher in an age of tolerance, liberalism and make way for a Divine Golden Age. Humphrey Davy of laughing gas fame hung out with Coleridge, Wordsworth and other Romantic types and explored the poetic as well as medical potential of his discoveries. William Crookes, with his pioneering work on the electron, did so in context of his parapsychological investigations into survival of human awareness after death…the list goes on.

Assembled by the knowledge discovered by the scientific project the industrial age trundles, hissing steam and belching smoke, onto the stage of history. Machines, chemical processes and even the beginnings of a science of the psyche were pressed into service by the elites to produce product. With two World Wars under its belt the military industrial complex could rise up and spread out; through emerging communication and transportation networks, through the new universality of shared clock time, through advertising and products, into every corner of the globe, every heart and every mind. But though the rulers of culture sought to harness this new discourse, to make it seem that all along they'd seen the sense of the scientific project, what they could not master was the Gnostic element that was essential to science itself, the desire embedded in it to know God (or the universe if you prefer) for oneself.

A clear example of this happened during World War II. On July 16, 1945 'the Gadget' was detonated in New Mexico, signalling the beginning of the atomic age. Two years before this Albert Hofmann had ushered in the entheogenic age with his accidental ingestion of LSD-25. As the atomic blast exploded outward so Hofmann's astonishingly powerful drug propelled him inward.

LSD was the first tremor in the latest wave of the Gnostic project. As dominant-dominator culture generated the terrifying spectre of atomic apocalypse, so the genie was about to escape from Hofmann's bottle and into the mind of Leary, Kesey, Huxley and millions of others. And this is inevitable because it's intrinsic to the process. The Gnostic quest, the personal exploration of mystery, demands that we use real, repeatable and personally engaging techniques to discover the world. Science is one expression of this experimental method, and entheogenics, the use of chemicals to explore our own minds is another. LSD and the wave of psychoactives that followed it, became woven into a new Invisible College, often simply called 'the Underground'. Informal networks of chemists, hipsters, heads, freaks and mystics, connected together through their use of these exotic materials.

The entheogenic revolution, as I'm sure we are all aware, was an essential component to many of the emerging technologies and ideas that have developed over the last sixty or so years. Space exploration, the ecological movement, computers, fractal mathematics and many more areas of human endeavour have been deeply informed by the use of entheogenic experience. These psychoactive materials, some discovered in far flung traditional cultures, others precipitated into crystal reality by modern alchemists, are to the mind as Galileo's telescope was to the heavens. By taking these materials into our bodies we can come to the realisation that our consciousness is capable of a rich, sometimes ecstatic, sometimes distressing, range of states.

We are moving from a state where we have one literal, normative awareness into a world in which awareness can be radically shifted, enhanced and explored.

Certainly there are dangers here. LSD was eagerly seized on as a possible weapon, just as information technology goes hand in hand with surveillance and control. But psychoactive drugs (particularly those we often call the psychedelics or entheogens) have a particular potency that I think is indicated by the fact that neither communist nor capitalist states have been able to incorporate them into the status quo. This is particularly intriguing in the case of capitalist cultures where one would normally expect such a valuable product to simply slot into the range of consumer choices we all enjoy. Aside of arguments about covert programs of black market racketeering, we are still in an age when, as the case of Casey Hardison demonstrates, one may spend more time in prison for manufacturing LSD than for killing someone.

Could it be that the entheogens occupy this strange outlaw place precisely because they are so deeply part of the Gnostic story? Scientifically derived and described chemicals that let us see God for ourselves. Could it be that, taken in a supportive environment and positive mind-set, these substances decondition us from literalism, from clinging on to monolithic dogma?

As we face the emergence of a new reality. A New World Order and Global Village, what are the teachings that many people derive from these entheogenic revelations? Sure these things are personal, subjective, but by building up a picture of many results we can come to know the common reality of these experiences. Mostly these experiences, in common with the majority of mystical states, point towards our common humanity. They remind us of our connection to the earth and invoke a compassion and humorous delight. They help us pay attention to the universe in a way that is unfettered by Thoth's Pharmakon but that does not abandon it. And though they have their own pitfalls they can help us drop our preconditioned preconceptions and to "...see things as they truly are, infinite."

Such states of modified awareness point away from the literal. From the received wisdom of text and towards the fact that if we want to understand God, we must look into the Book of Nature. Certainly writing informs us and can help us share our discoveries and test them in the mutual space of society. But now we can see the Pharmakon for what it is, a poison or medicine, it's only the dosage; our approach to writing, that determines the effect. This reorientation to text, and an emphasis on lived experience, is the basis of the Gnostic project. It frees our imagination, and as Terence McKenna said; "All of these things are taking hold, and not a moment too soon."

Return to Chaos

So what exactly is this Chaos Magick thing all about? This year the premier organisation that espouses this style, The Magical Pact of the Illuminates of Thanateros (IOT) will host the Colours of Chaos event in London. Moreover the IOT is celebrating its 30th birthday. So is Chaos Magick (CM) dead or alive? What does this approach have to offer? Has Chaos gone mainstream? And what, quite frankly, has Chaos Magick ever done for you? Naturally what follows here is just my opinion about Chaos Magick, I'm sure you, gentle reader, have your own ideas...

The Chaos Magick approach, as the briefest glance at Wikipedia will reveal originated in the British Isles during the late 1970s. The chief protagonists included Ray Sherwin, author of, among other works, *The Book of Results* (1978), and Pete Carroll, author of *Liber Null* (1978). This year sees the publication of another work by Carroll *The Apophenion*, marking another turning point in the development of Chaos Magick. Pete retired from active membership of the IOT in 1995, and has been quietly pursuing his own research. Latterly however he has been spotted teaching on courses organised by Robert Anton Wilson's (RAW) Maybe Logic Academy, and Pete has recently initiated the on-line occult university Arcanorium College (www.arcanoriumcollege.com).

The connection with RAW, co-author of *The Illuminatus! Trilogy* (1975) is important. Chaos Magick since its inception has delighted in the Taoist influenced crazy wisdom portrayed in *Illuminatus!* Eris, Goddess of discord is worshipped, global mega corporations are brought to their knees by tiny acts of humorous insurgency. Those who seek to guide the development of human evolution have gotta be prepared to stare the cosmic joke in the face and have a bloody good laugh.

So what is the CM style that Pete Carroll and his colleagues (including many of those tutors on the Arcanorium College courses) have developed? What is Chaos Magick? Naturally there are many possible answers to this question. The Chaos approach has been characterised by a Do It Yourself ethic. Rather than rely on sacred texts or apostolic succession, Chaos Magick privileges personal experience and experiment. In some respects we might reply "so what?" Lots of contemporary witches, Pagans and occultists profess this approach and will happily describe themselves as 'eclectic'. Perhaps this is, in some measure, a clear vindication of the Chaoist agenda; allow me to provide an example from my own experience.

Back in the 1980s (those heady days of Thatcherism and the Peace Convoy) I was involved in an 'experimental' Wiccan coven. We were experimental in that we didn't use the formal initiation system of three degrees (though we did develop a comprehensive training programme for members to follow). We also departed from the 'traditional' words of the Gardnerian/Alexandrian *Book of Shadows*. We created our own Sabbat rituals, in a sense developing the expansion of the conventional Wiccan tradition that can be seen in Stewart and Janet Farrar's *Eight Sabbats for Witches* (1981). In short, we evolved our own ritual approach but we still kept our experimentation, in broad terms, within the framework of Wicca. We restructured the Wheel of the Year and the mythic births, deaths and re-births that the seasonal cycle suggested. We retained the traditional circle casting procedure but modified the words. We distilled complex rituals into what we felt were more immediate forms of dramatic ritual. We also made some tentative steps towards linking the Wheel of the Year with Tantric practices (see *Seeds of Magick 1990*). Many other witches in our community (also predominantly of the Gardnerian/Alexandrian school) were involved in ceremonial magick. Alexandrian Wicca in particular has always had a close association with Qabalah. However other traditions; shamanism, the Northern tradition, Eastern practices – these things were still at the outer limits of many witches' worlds. Although there was syncretism of traditions there was also a fair amount of time spent worrying about authenticity (who initiated whom) and the boundaries of The Craft and other practices. The New Age movement was the shadow of Wicca; all white light and wishy-washy. Eastern magick only impinged into Wicca in the form of the chakra system. Other styles were given less respect. I recall one prominent Wiccan talking about shamanism to me and professing the belief that the first four letters of the word (i.e. 'sham') said something about those who claimed to practice this form of magick.

Now, in the early 21st century, especially among younger occultists and pagans, those divisions that haunted late 20th century occultism (for example left verses right hand path techniques, Eastern vs. Western occultism) have been blown out of the water. A pervasive eclecticism and the powerful transdisciplinary viewpoint of Google has created a complex, deeply intertwined magickal blend of occultisms.

Of course the 'traditional witch' (or Hermetic mystic, or Asatru or whatever) might well decry this process. Undoubtedly there are those who see this blending of styles and approaches as a deviation from the One True Tradition. Fortunately, more and more people simply don't give that kind of nonsense the time of day. We all know by now that any tradition; any magickal style is widely syncretic. Attempts to get to the 'pure source' of any teaching inevitably flounder on the simple fact that, as social beings, humans have always mixed genes, language, cultures and deities.

So Chaos Magick was (and perhaps still is) one of the approaches at the vanguard of this interweaving of traditions. But what else is it about?

Like the title of Ray Sherwin's *The Book of Results*, Chaos Magick is about getting results, and real results require real effort. Let me give an example from the element of Chaos praxis known as 'paradigm shifting'. If you're going to explore a 'paradigm' (i.e. an approach to the world) you need to really get into it. Superficial surfing the net isn't the same as plunging into the waters of the noosphere and immersing yourself in a practice. So rather than the eclecticism of blending traditions resulting in a bland, uncritical clouds of pipe dreams, what you get is some seriously well trained adepts. For instance if you're going to get to know the runes you (probably) need to make your own set, stain them with your blood, spend at least 24 days getting to know the song, posture and magickal energies of each letter in the Futhark and ideally hang yourself from a tree for at least one night. Then you need to start working seriously with them. Adopting the runic paradigm isn't just about buying a set of pre-packaged rune stones and doing a few readings for your mates. It's about using these magickal letters to accomplish your Will, getting properly inside that paradigm to learn how they work. Thus the Chaos Magick style encourages depth as well as diversity. Sure you can aim for a 'working knowledge' of many systems but those that the Chaos Magician chooses to explore they will really get into. This type of full immersion in a paradigm is, in part, about the process of discovering technique. The

Chaos Magician might be quite impressed by your hand-tooled copy of the Necronomicon as an art object, but what they really want to know is 'what tricks does it do?' This thirst for discovering new techniques leads Chaos Magickians outside of the explicitly occult discourse. You're just as likely to spot a Chaos Magician leafing through a book on NLP or management psychology as perusing the Mind, Body and Spirit section of the local bookstore.

Okay but what about the whole hierarchy thing? How come such a fiercely independent, anarchic sounding approach can spawn organised groups like the Illuminates of Thanateros?

My involvement with the IOT has only come in the last five years. I'd hung out with Dave Lee, Pete Carroll and Phil Hine in the 1980s but never really wanted to sign up to the Order. I suppose like many people I found the notion of a Chaos Magick Order a strange one – if we are all adepts and all doing our own thing should we need the trappings of degrees, passwords and hierarchy? In my Coven we experimented with various non-hierarchical, consensus based systems of organisation, with variable levels of success. What was the point of Pete Carroll's 'hierarchical gambit?' – Well, now I know.

The IOT operates a series of degrees that represent commitment to the organisation (not magickal advancement per se) and has a system of Insubordinates to continuously challenge those in positions of authority within the network (again see dear ol' Wikipedia for the full details). The vast majority of members stay at the 3rd degree (Initiate). These members are the core of the network and form the vast majority of participants. A third degree member might be very active for years and then decide to step back to pursue research outside the IOT structure (perhaps by disappearing within a selected paradigm for a while). They may need to step back from attending meetings temporarily because of academic, family or any number of other commitments. That same member is then very welcome to re-appear later (especially if they come bearing gifts of some nifty new techniques to share) and would hope to plug into the on-going IOT story. One of the roles of the 2nd and 1st degree members is to ensure that the network structure is kept alive and well so that 3rd degree members can do their own thing, knowing that the antiarchy persists which they may return to when they Will.

And this, for me, is the whole point of the IOT and indeed the Chaos Magick approach in general. It is about creating a creative dialogue between the individual and the collective. Each person is actively involved in their own research and development. This process is one that requires a meaningful personal commitment. This is the Great Work after all. But as we discover techniques, as we learn new approaches we bring these back to the collective space. The general model for any Chaos Magick, and certainly IOT meeting, is that each person brings a contribution of Work. This can vary from a series of yoga asanas they have been working on; it might be a psychotherapeutic practice, through to full-blown ceremonial ritual. The person bringing the technique needs to know their stuff sufficiently to communicate what they know with confidence and passion. Through this method both the teacher or ritual leader and the rest of the group are enriched. Sometimes techniques are developed or explored in working groups collectively. But whether the acquisition of new ideas is from an individual or a group, sooner or later there is a duty to pass this knowledge on. This emphasis on transmitting technique means that in a very short space of time an organisation like the IOT can, collectively, have engaged with a large number of occult styles and developed excellence in a high proportion of those approaches. In practical terms this is another reason for the Orderly structure of the IOT. This process of formulating a magickal Order as a 'learning organisation' means a wide range of techniques can be explored vigorously. Security systems, including oaths and a mentored trial period before formal initiation, attempt to maintain safety for both the network and the individual. Powerful forces (dah! dah! dah!) are abroad in the temples of the Chaos Magician so it's important that all personnel can cope with that intensity.

Chaos Magick has accelerated the blending of different magickal currents. It has created an approach that demands real work rather than armchair occultism. It seeks diversity and depth and a clear understanding of technique that can be passed on to enrich the magickal development of others. Chaos Magick, with its love of contemporary culture, DIY style and crazy wisdom, also manages to retain the humour that informed its Discordian genesis in the 1970s. All this in only 30 years, and I guarantee that, far from being dead, Chaos Magick has only just got started!

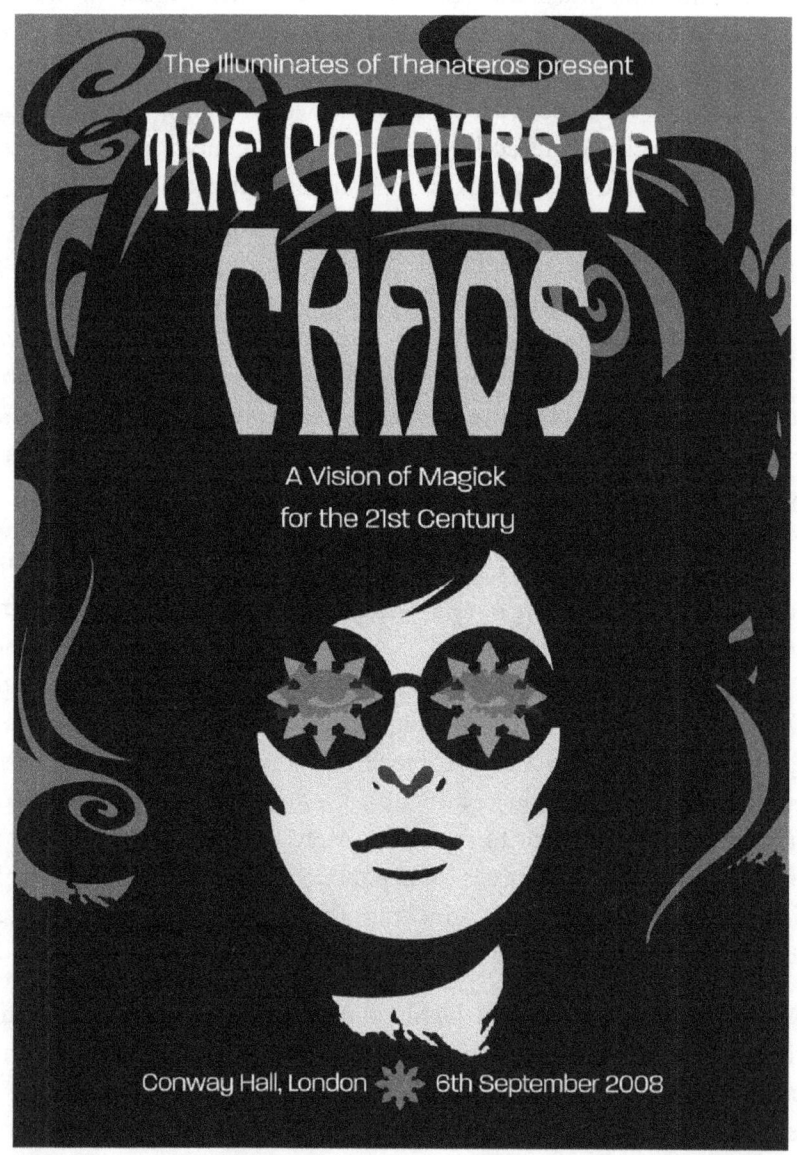

Fig 8 Flyer for *The Colours of Chaos*

A Crisis of Chaos

> Do we want to remain big people in a tiny world or to become a little people in a vaster world? - Fred Hoyle

The relationship between the individual, magick and wider culture

"Why Chaos Magick?" Asked a friend at a talk I gave recently. He complained that with all the email he had to answer and the apparent confusion in his world chaos was the last thing he needed. And it's true. For many of us humans it is structure, order that we crave. Moreover isn't Chaos Magick a kind of contradiction in terms? The magician is a figure of power and what power is there in a life fractured by chaos?

In many respects this is true. Chaos Magick does seek to stir us up. Chaos Magick aims to destabilise many aspects of the congenial reality that we seek (though seldom accomplish). A typical Chaos Magick gathering will see methods being deployed that engage a number of different esoteric styles. Perhaps more importantly this heady cocktail of practices may also employ radically different beliefs. One moment you're engaged in a Buddhist meditation on compassion, the next you're cursing someone. One can also attend to the biography of (Chaos) magicians. These people seldom have easy and straightforward lives. Why is this? Again if magick is about power, how come the sad magicians don't simply cast a sigil to make themselves happy again?

In order to understand this apparent paradox, or built in self-destruct mechanism, we need to appreciate the wider purpose of magick.

Let's consider our lives as individuals. What we can be certain about is that all our plans, all our accomplishments, all our striving will end in death. We are born as awareness embedded in a matrix of flesh that will undoubtedly wither. However we also know that, as each new consciousness comes on-line, it is born into a web that consists of the sum total of all the other minds that have gone before it. We are the ancestors of the future, our being-in-the-world, gives rise to structures in the noosphere that persist, potentially, long after our hearts and lungs give out.

How does magick fit into this? When we step back and consider our species (or perhaps the whole field of consciousness which may well underlie all reality) can we make sense of what it means to be a magician? Is it possible to create an evolutionary psychological model of why magicians exist?

Essential to understanding the activity of the magician is a greater sense of what we, as thinking beings are. In day-to-day life we commonly identify ourselves with our egos, that strident 'I' that wants and desires and fears. It is of course essential that we generate ego-I awareness. This is the sense of self that permits us to look at the reflection in the mirror and exclaim 'oh my God! Look at the state of my hair!' Yet the ego-I is far from the whole story. Intellectually we may recognise that we are a swarming legion of unconscious processes, minuscule cellular interactions and grand narrative DNA programming. Take for example the reaction to the cry of a child. This can galvanise a whole host of responses in our somatic self that the ego-I has a devil of a job to ignore. Trying to blot out our biological responses to our fellow humans is a process that the military spend millions of dollars on. Give a human a gun and, typically, they will fail to pull the trigger, sometimes even when they are clearly in mortal danger. Rooky soldiers miss all the time. Our DNA cries out for different ways of resolving disputes so loudly that it takes exhaustive training to overcome these and create the cold, hard heart of the automatic killer.

Yet our tenacious ego will leap back into the driving seat at the earliest opportunity. When we perform acts of great courage, rescuing someone from a burning car, we explain we just acted. Yet later our ego sneaks back in and tries to build up the fantasy that it (I, me) am a hero. Equally we talk about choosing to have children as though it is a simply rational (egoic) decision. Rather than acknowledge the great pressure from biology to reproduce (sometimes in the most difficult and inappropriate of circumstances) we tell ourselves that we 'chose' to get pregnant. This is perhaps particularly in evidence in the modern Western world in which, although we understand more about our unconscious processes than ever before, choice is everything.

So what is the relationship of magick to the ego? The first thing to understand is that the desire to be a magician arises naturally in our species. This desire may attach itself to practices, ways of engaging with the Mystery, that we clearly recognise as esoteric. Funny stars drawn on the floor, incantations, and chambers flooded with incense; you get the picture. But this desire also emerges in people we would more often describe as artists.

Artists, like magicians are compelled to do their work. They may find favour in wider culture and end up rich, but they can just as easily end up in some damp garret starving to death. Perhaps art and magick arise from the same neurological patterning, and will someday be clearly identified. The ego of the magician, of the artist, may wish to stop. They may try. But they cannot. This pattern is embedded too deep; one might as well ask them to stop breathing.

So according egoic concerns to magick ("why don't they just do spells to get mega rich?") is to miss the point. Because magicians certainly have their own egos but it is not these that motivate their work. The role of the magician is importantly a cultural one. Artists have been described as the 'antenna of culture' and this is an excellent analogy. Like artists, magicians are those people who are blessed (or doomed) to be part of the sensory system of our species. Magicians are those who are seeking out 'the Mystery', the unknown, and as such dwell in the same place as those who are compelled to investigate the underlying patterns of the universe (scientists), or the realm of possible forms (artists). The purpose of magick (as with science and art) is that the process of experiment generates waves in the noosphere that influence wider culture. In the case of science this process is obvious; I experiment with certain objects and make observations, eventually I arrive at the underlying principles of, say, electro-magnetism. Finally a new technology pops into culture. In the case of art the process may seem more haphazard and less generally applicable. So what Andy Warhol ever done for me then? Well art both crystallises culture (Warhol crystallised the notion of mass reproduction as a form of beauty) and expands it (Warhol made art of simply filming the Statue of Liberty). Art (as a pure praxis) in the past was typically subordinate to the paymasters of the artist. Religious art is commissioned by Popes, banners are produced depicting noble workers, funded by The Party. However each artist puts their own spin on even the most tedious commission. Moreover hidden away in studios, scattered on the floor, are innumerable sketches, experiments, explorations which only in recent times have we allowed to emerge as fully functioning artworks.

The magician is different. What does he or she make? There are several possible answers to this. In one respect the magician seeks to discover the currents that flow through the noosphere in exactly the same way that the scientist seeks the hidden laws, or the artist the impetus to found a new 'movement'. These currents are at once deeply personal and also collective, for they interpenetrate all minds. The magician seeks to deploy gnosis and belief to influence (or perhaps blend with in the sense that the Aikido player blends with their opponent) these things. There are several purposes to magical work, none of which are watertight compartments. A magician may seek to understand the nature of time, they might seek to accomplish personal transformation or perhaps heal the wounded. But in all cases the important point is not the apparent purpose (or indeed outcome) of the magical act. Instead what matters is the magician's discernment of the currents in the noosphere. Such sensitivity is akin to that which a sailor has. Smelling the wind and being wise to its direction is what permits the mariner to move as desired. What cargo the vessel is carrying (the payload if you will of the trance or sigil) is in some respects immaterial. It is the ability to read the wind and waves that matters.

Nowhere is this more apparent than in the nature of so-called 'results magick'. Experienced sorcerers are all familiar with the three ways as act of magick can go. It can work, it can do nothing, or it can backfire. Surely we wouldn't want to use a gun that exhibited these features? So the trick comes in learning the rhythms and patterns that are hidden in the noosphere. A magickal event, like an artistic creation, *arises* as much as it is planned. This explains why in many cases the result of a ritual can manifest well before the ceremony is enacted. This also explains why even the most experienced magician can find that, however much their ego wants something, that something is unlikely to be attained if the unconscious tides are pushing against it. In this sense the magician can be said not so much to do magick as to ensure that the magick of the universe is done. The wizard is the medium for something much larger than egocentric desires. They are the vectors by which the Mystery becomes revealed to culture.

In esoteric language this situation is often expressed in terms of the (True) Will. To be in a place of power, the occultist acts in the only way he or she must and no other. In the same way the genius (or dæmon) of the artist reveals itself *just so*. In fact sometimes this process can be pretty hard on the human vehicle of that spirit. The artist, like the magician can be torn apart. Cultural duties, norms and expectations can suffocate this outpouring. Our genius is tortured, mad and excluded from polite society. Rarely do such individuals find themselves in positions of temporal power in historic cultures (except occasionally in their guise as messianic cult leaders). The skills we value in our leaders are not generally those of divine madness. Instead we tend to select individuals who are committed to the ego-I field of social interactions. There are of course exceptions to this, both in 'traditional cultures' and in those wiser States where magicians were also the viziers of political rulers (such as Ancient Egypt).

The model of the dæmon illustrates the situation of the magician admirably. The dæmon demands to be listened to, and, though the artist may be trapped in insanity (as Richard Dadd) or addiction (Crowley), it will not be denied. The wise magician gives himself up to his dæmon but does so through the process of continuously 'cleansing' the vehicle (the self) through which the dæmon manifests. Repeated practice of bodywork, entheogenic use, banishing rituals etc create the optimum conditions for the dæmon's manifestation, and aim to bring the ego into alignment with the Will.

Naturally, give the slings and arrows of experience there are times for the magician when the demands of the dæmon seem to vigorously oppose societal norms. Such crises can lead to insanity and even death. To smash these kleshas we must employ all our resources, alone. And this is where the chaos comes in. Not simply as the supermarket of belief but as the living force or outpouring power. Embracing this can be the hardest of all tests but there is no choice for the magician. As Nietzsche teaches "One must have chaos in oneself in order to give birth to a dancing star."

The Black Flag & The Mystery

Anarchy in the Everyday

Anarchy is an appealing idea. The notion of a situation, or perhaps process, of existing without an external ruler. What would this look like, how would it feel? Anarchist discourse, from my own reading, typically places a great emphasis on the negation of power; this is, to give a simple derivation an = without archy = rule, after all. It is defined by what it is not, and in such circumstances perhaps it may be difficult for us to see what anarchism might positively be?

I suppose I'd better start by declaring my own position, it may help make things clearer and may allow you, gentle reader, to be more generous with your critique of me if my political analysis fails to meet your own high standards. I suspect that I'm an anarchist but this is a political and social outgrowth of my own core project, which I usually describe as magick.

Magick (however one chooses to spell it) is an approach to human experience that seeks to explore 'the Mystery', ie that which is occult (hidden, repressed, excluded). As an approach it uses methods for changing consciousness such as trance techniques, drugs, sex, art and other techniques to uncover what may be possible beyond our current human experience.

So anarchism for me is one such possibility with the Mystery, a delicious, inviting idea about the reformulation of social relations that comes from a radically different place than many of the systems of social organisation (theocracy, communism, capitalism etc.) that our species has explored (especially in the context of large groups or 'states').

I'm always very impressed when I see, in various ways, what anarchism as a lived-in philosophy creates. Those islands of anarchist culture I'm familiar with; from Spain, South America, ancient Taoist China – these places, quite frankly, sound amazing. Nothing heartens me more than the facts that behind the barricades people rapidly set up schools, hospitals, cultivate food and care for their neighbours with autonomous activity, consensus process, and often an evident delight. These zones demonstrate to me how much anarchism is about the ideas of justice and fairness. Most anarchists I know are thoroughly good people, they are amongst some of the most sensitive and moral individuals I have met. However reading a journal like *325* or *For Nothing Against Everything* one might easily come away with other impressions.

The violence of anarchism; hooded figures chucking petrol bombs, is the surface level, one that understandably will distress many people. But such direct action springs from a position vastly different to that of much State, and indeed certain 'terrorist', violence.

The anarchist, like the magician, is involved in a spiritual journey. Spiritual in the sense that, like the alchemical notion of spirit (as the product of the four elements of fire, water, earth and air) it is a holistic reformulation of the self and its relationship to others. The rich darkness from which these reformulations spring is, I feel, elegantly symbolised by the Black Flag.

Initially the Black Flag, like the negative definitions of anarchism, is a species of koan. (A paradoxical anecdote or a riddle that has no solution; used in Taoism & Zen Buddhism to show the inadequacy of logical reasoning.) We advance on the Parliament building, burning and looting as we go, and still, like our enemy, we are waving flags. Yet these pennants are black, faceless, or perhaps more accurately, containing all colours as dark potential. They are like the black soil of ancient Egypt (the 'Black Land' from which 'black' magick originates), seething with fecundity, with limitless possibility. The Black Flag is both symbol and anti-symbol, refusing to limit itself to one idea, one glyph; it contains and absorbs all possible frequencies of light.

Like organs such as *325* the Black Flag becomes an axis mundi around which anarchists and fellow travellers can rally. It marks off an environment where the rules of social engagement are different – namely that there are no externally imposed rules. Into these environments stories can pour and be heard. *325* regularly carries tales of remarkable human fortitude and courage in the face of acts of oppression. These are stories that are heard very little in wider culture and stories that it takes some work to understand. The story of the bank robbery is in fact only a tiny part of a much larger process, which the readers of *325* will typically appreciate.

But when we are not storming the Parliament building? What happens to our anarchism then? How is it manifested? The key idea for me is that of the *attentat*. In essence this is the idea of taking responsibility for one's own actions, specifically in terms of acts of political violence or terrorism, especially a political assassination.

In the recent riots in Greece that led to the death of three bank workers what was telling was the way the people involved in the action mourned and took responsibility for these deaths. In this sense the anarchist position is a heroic one; autonomously (without bowing to outside cultural pressure to behave in a certain manner) we take responsibility for our own power and our use of that power. This is what, in Western magical parlance, is referred to as pursuing the course of one's 'true Will'. That's why, to me and perhaps the even less trained ear, anarchist literature can seem like National Socialist propaganda. We have the heroic image of the anarchist standing in opposition to the tyranny of the faceless State. Our rebel needs to be strong, resolute and to thrive on a diet of his or her sovereign individualist praxis. The anarchist riots, clear in the knowledge they have the power to kill in doing so. But they are heroes; they have broken their mind-forged manacles and, whatever the personal cost, demand change.

However it's the deeply felt desire for social justice, a desire that runs so deep it must get beneath and overturn the status quo; this makes anarchism quite different from National Socialism (and indeed many other political projects). Anarchists care about the world, care about human relationships and in fact their autonomous being is critically embedded within a community. In a telling conversation, with two anarchist friends, who are very familiar with the shooting by police of Alexandros Grigoropoulos in Athens in 2008, they were unable to recall the names of the officers responsible for the murder. Anarchists are against the police, the social dynamic that they represent and enforce; their anger is vented at these roles, not directly at the individual humans who find themselves perpetuating these power relations. The anarchist rebellion is against a culture of violence and repression and isn't fixated on the specific perpetrators. The names of the assailants are unimportant, it is the act of violence as demonstrated through the structures of repressive policing that are at fault. Our anarchist hero riots not to kill people but to destroy the culture that enslaves them.

In terms of the 'magical project'. By transforming ourselves we transform our relationships in the world, these in turn transform who we are and help us reach out towards The Mystery – what it may be possible for us to become. Our focus is on the relationships we sustain, oppose and seek to cultivate. We accept our responsibility for this work of transformation and refuse simplistic demonisation of others; instead we work to change the fundamental process of relationship. In this sense the political position of anarchism is the magical process of transformation as it appears in the social domain.

The transformations of self and context celebrated in *325* are typically those of the fire and air (again to use alchemical language). Fire is destruction, purification and energy – it is manifest as bombs, looting and burning tyres in the streets. Air in this case is about division, communication and information – it is manifest as imprisonment, communiques and discussion. So where is the earth and the water in our model? It is in the processes that happen behind the barricades. It is the opening of social centres, the collectivisation of food production, the gentle collaborative efforts of men, women and children to realise a new culture.

In everyday terms these gentle arts of subversion seek to generate new realities. They do so by fundamentally reorienting our own relationship with power. Power of course isn't a thing, it is an activity, it exists only in its deployment but it's easy to internalise the assumed power that (State) authority has over us. By doing so we fall quickly into patterns of social interaction that prop up the regimes that we deplore.

Allow me to give an example not from the sharp end of radical insurrection but from a simple event in daily life. I work in a museum and recently there was a group of teenagers hanging around the entrance to the building. It was the end of the school holidays and this group of people (of around 10-14 years of age) were bored. Riding their bikes and scooters around the paved area outside the entrance, they were shouting to each other, laughing and smoking. My colleagues were getting nervous, feeling their space invaded by this rowdy mob. I went outside and asked them to please keep their bikes away from the entrance so that they didn't hit anyone coming out. They yelled back a species of agreement and I went away.

Less than ten minutes later they were riding close to the door again. My boss started making preparations to call the town centre security to get these kids moved on. At the time I was, ironically, drafting a document aimed to helping young people engage more directly with the museums in the region. I sat behind my desk and wrote, while I could hear the kids yelling and my boss trying to figure out how to use the radio to summon the law.

Then, without any consideration, I went outside. I took my notes with me and sat with the youth on the steps by the entrance. Again I asked them to keep their bikes away from the doorway. I continued my work and made some small talk. Within less than 10 minutes I was engaged in an interesting conversation with these people. One young man told me how he was shown in a photograph on display in the museum. I was able to ask various questions about their use of social media that really helped my research. In the end many of them left for the nearby park but a couple said they'd come back later to check the museum out.

My boss had observed what I was doing and had decided not to summon the security. She had also taken the opportunity to modify her relationship with the power dynamics in the situation.

So what happened here? The first point is that I acted spontaneously. I didn't plan this out in my head. I wasn't manipulating them I was just acting in a way that felt right at the time. Rather than re-enforce the 'us vs. them' boundary by involving the security services I'd stepped across the boundary. Made a connection, de-stabilised the 'obvious' power relations that could have emerged in this interaction. No kids were distressed by being bawled out by a burley security guard, and my museum didn't get a brick through the window from an aggrieved youth. In fact all of us ended up richer for this event. The kids talked to me about my job, I talked to them about their school. We learnt from each other, and perhaps formed the basis for future solidarity.

For me, for all of us, each day there are thousands of opportunities for us to explore the Mystery, and in a political sense this means to take up the Black Flag and engage with the project of our own anarchism. Simply put we allow ourselves to own our own power, to challenge social relationships where power is imaged as being 'outside and imposed' and instead see the opportunities to transform social relationships in the here and now. This process manifests itself in the interactions between parents and children, lover and beloved, police and protestor, and in each of these interactions we have the possibility of breaking the program of externalised power, changing our relationships in a way that is both heroic for us as individuals and supportive in realising a society of greater freedom for all people.

Personally I don't care if our future as a species is an anti-civilisation re-immersion in wilderness existence or if it's a high tech, low impact journey to explore the stars. What matters are the social relationships that exist in any of these possible futures. It's quite possible to have a small-scale tribal egalitarian culture that demonstrates terrifying levels of cruelty; it's also possible to have complex civilisations predicated on mutual aid and environmental sensitivity (for examples please see my essay on Utopia & Armageddon in *Magick Works*). What matters is the process of understanding our own social power ('know thyself') and feeling the right way to deploy this to create the fair and just world we want to inhabit ('to thine own self be true').

In this way we may come to live in an anarchist world; one in which nothing is true (imposed from the outside) and everything is permitted.

The Gratuitous Grace

The son of the sea is born

The front room in my cottage is full of women. Two are friends, one is my partner, and the other two are midwives. A red blanket is spread on the ground; I knew it would be red. Provided by one of the friends in this room (one of Helen's birth partners, a lovely local Druid lady) it was one of those quirks of precognition. A red blanket. I knew it would be like this. Helen keeps talking until finally her movements on the birthing ball change and she feels it happening. She is open and the baby is coming. She cries, "It feels different this time". I reassure her "that's because your body knows what to do".

Blood, sound, a breath. My second son is born.

Dylan, son of the sea, you are my gratuitous grace, your smile gladdens my heart, your demonstrative love is a constant source of delight. More than this you an object lesson in a very simple fact; that we are divided for love's sake but that love itself does not divide. My love for my first son isn't weakened by your arrival. You are not some problematic 'entry of the third' but rather another unique person for me to get to know. I have fallen in love with you, as I did with your brother, the moment you were born. You do not diminish my love for anyone else but rather support and enrich it.

Ah, if only adult polyamory were so easy! As easy as loving all our children can be.

Lessons from the Witches

'Museums enable people to explore collections for inspiration, learning and enjoyment. They are institutions that collect, safeguard and make accessible artefacts and specimens, which they hold in trust for society.'

- Museums Association Definition

The Boscastle Museum of Witchcraft houses so many wonderful exhibits. Allow me to introduce you to some of my favourites. The first one is to be found in the deepest recesses of the first floor. This catalogue entry for this object at www.museumofwitchcraft.com describes it thus:

Fig 9. Museum Number: 900. Object Name: Figure with chair and staff

Physical Description: Life-size goat-headed (Baphomet) figure wearing a white robe, and with a candle between his horns, holding a forked staff and seated on an elaborately carved chair.

Museum Classification: Horned God

Size: 1350 x 750 x 750 mm (approx)

It was this evocative figure that I recall encountering as a child as I browsed the plates in the coffee table occult books that were popular in the 1970s. Redolent of hidden cults and their mysterious rites, this image exerted a magnetic fascination for me. Many years later I was to find myself dressed in the costume of this horned deity performing a ritual atop the fourth plinth in Trafalgar Square. As part of Andrew Gormely's art project I was selected as one of the 2400 participants that contributed to fill the plinth through several months in 2009. From meditating on this figure as a young man I had become Baphomet in the centre of the city, to raise the profile of the world-class collection that is now housed in The Witchcraft Museum.

By a curious twist of fate I did this as someone who, for the last eight years, has worked as a museum professional. My specialist area is the use of museum objects for learning. This may be the conventional type of educational work that museums often undertake (encouraging visits by school parties, college students and so forth), as well as more experimental work using museum objects in therapeutic contexts (particularly with people recovering from mental illness). (You can find out about some of the techniques I use in my book *Wonderful Things*.)

For me, both as a museum worker and especially as a practising occultist, the Boscastle collection is a rich source of interest and inspiration. Its collection ranges from ancient examples of charms drawn in yellowing parchment, through to ritual paraphernalia donated by contemporary practitioners. These objects are the material trances left by a whole series of interwoven human activities; community scapegoating, spells of protection for women in childbirth, the remnants of attempts to contact spirits, and much more.

Walking around the museum is an opportunity to explore objects that cluster around some of the most mysterious aspects of our humanity.

DEEP MAGIC

Why do we do magick? How is magick understood by the culture in which it appears? What methods do we employ to harness the hidden powers of the universe to do our bidding?

We all believe in magick, even those of us who profess to a scientific and rational frame of mind. For magick is the technology of the imagination, it is used to cure and curse and the processes that it employs are as ubiquitous as the placebo effect. There are amulets in this collection that accompanied soldiers fighting in the first mechanised conflict of the First World War. There are charms for curing livestock and evidence of divinatory systems that would help the querent negotiate the changing fortunes of life.

As we meet each object in the collection we are seeing the material echo of a complex web of stories. Here is one powerful example;

Fig 10. Museum Number: 40, Object Name: Curse

Physical Description: Black and white photograph of young woman, pierced with pins.

Other Object Name: Photograph

Museum Classification: Curses

Information: Original text by Cecil Williamson: 'this lucky find, found tucked away in the back of a local government office filing cabinet, speaks for itself. Someone had a cause to punish the nice looking lady secretary. One wonders what it was - dislike, envy, or a lover's quarrel. Liskeard, 1948.'

What led to the construction of this disturbing artefact? How did the creator(s) of this curse imagine that it would work? And of course the big question, what happened after this spell was cast? Given the period from which this object dates what knowledge informed this charm? The creation of images and their ceremonial destruction is certainly a technique that is documented as far back as the ancient Egyptian civilisation. But this is not to say that the sorcerer who laid this curse need have known that. Indeed the idea of ripping apart and destroying a photograph of someone you hate is an obvious symbolic act. But this object speaks not simply of an act of anger. This was a premeditated, planned event; there is method in this malice.

Of course the person who undertook this magical act was doing something illegal. If the date of 1948 is accurate then Witchcraft Act of 1735 was still in force. But this law, as with the later Fraudulent Mediums act of 1951, was concerned not with punishing malefic magick but with preventing con artists claiming supernatural power from earning any cash from their activities. If this spell was cast by someone on behalf of another, and especially if they gained financially from that process, they could be in serious trouble.

Before the 1735 legislation the position was very different. Acts of malefic magick would be punishable in themselves with the distinct possibility of execution for those convicted of such crimes.

The Witchcraft Museum collection, as well as being about magick, is also distinctly about how broader society responds to this process. The witch-hunts of the early modern period have furnished us with some of the grizzliest items in the museum collection. Take this example;

Fig 11. Museum Number: 161

Object Name: Scold's Bridle

Museum Classification: Persecution

Information: Scold's or Witch's Bridle: These brutal devices were really used to extract confessions from women. In 1591 Agnes Sampson of Berwick, Scotland 'was pinned to the wall of her cell by an iron witch's bridle, which had four sharp prongs that were forced into her mouth, against her tongue and cheeks...' Agnes eventually confessed to witchcraft and was strangled and burned. Original text by Cecil Williamson: 'scolds' bridles such as this were used on witches when they were paraded, stripped naked to the waist and whipped through the town. The purpose of the bridle was to prevent the witch shouting and cursing the town or persons in authority.'

Whether the curse from 1948 was successful is anyone's guess but ducking stools, thumbscrews and the scold's bridle most certainly were.

For me this is why it's fantastic that this museum is one of 'witchcraft' because the word 'witch' points not only to the modern neo-Pagan religion but also to the lethal power that a culture can exercise, often on the flimsiest of evidence, against its citizens. The Boscastle Museum of Witchcraft collection documents of how we humans can turn against each other, especially in times of trouble and turmoil. This is not simply a quaint collection of outmoded folk belief or New Age paraphernalia, but a testament to those people who were executed for the crime of being a witch. It serves as a timely reminder that the most powerful curses come not from isolated sorcerers but often from our community leaders. Long may this collection inspire, entrance and entertain, and may it also cast its own spell for (in the words of the plaque in Exeter, commemorating the last English women to be hanged for witchcraft) '…an end to persecution and intolerance'.

Wine & Strange Drugs

I am the Snake that giveth Knowledge & Delight and bright glory, and stir the hearts of men with drunkenness. To worship me take wine and strange drugs whereof I will tell my prophet, & be drunk thereof! They shall not harm ye at all. It is a lie, this folly against self. The exposure of innocence is a lie. Be strong, o man! lust, enjoy all things of sense and rapture: fear not that any God shall deny thee for this. I am alone: there is no God where I am

In this channelled text, *The Book of the Law*, Aleister Crowley is repeating something that has been at the heart of most esoteric traditions since the first shaman sat, pupils dilated, on the African savannah surrounded by lots of bluish tinged mushrooms. Drugs, those fantastic alchemical materials that can catalyse heaven or hell, are the key ingredients of many magickal systems. Where would the witch be without her cauldron of solanaceae? Where would the shaman be without his power plants? Where would the alchemist be without the philosopher's stone, or the druid without those droplets of inspiration?

Crowley famously soaked himself in 'cognac, cunt and cocaine'. He plunged into plant induced altered states, following a trajectory that propelled magick out of the doldrums of the post medieval and into the modern age. Uncle Aleister and many of his contemporaries were interested in exploring consciousness through chemical means. Crowley played around with opiates, cocaine, and hashish and was a pioneer explorer of peyote. He made good use of these chemicals in his rituals, famously spiking the audience at his Rites of Eleusis with mescaline. Crowley wanted to generate a 'religious ecstasy' in attendees, a project that was at the core of his mission to promote the cult of Thelema. The Rites of Eleusis aimed to transform the Victorian ladies and gentlemen in London's Caxton Hall, into modern Pagans. Pagans because their God would be the intoxicating spirit of personal revelation, mediated by artistic ritual, fuelled by mind-altering substances.

Today, although the post-Protestant world is full of Pagans and magicians and witches, an engagement with these sacred medicines is often curiously absent, at least overtly. Let's take the example of Wicca (a system with some of its roots in Crowley's magick), is this a Dionysian, ecstatic Pagan cult? In a word, no. Instead most of its rituals are little more than a titillating (though at times engaging) Co-Freemasonry where, although *The Book of Shadows* suggests the use of psychoactives, these are painfully absent from the ceremonies of many Wiccans. However within the more outré groups, such as Thee Temple ov Psychick Youth, some freestyle shamanic practitioners, and many people who would call themselves Thelemites or Chaos magicians, 'chemognosis' is alive and well.

And it's not as though we've got a shortage of these things. Indeed on a planet where we're used to hearing about species going extinct, in the wonderful world of psychoactives, new ones seem to be being discovered every week. Not only do we have all those novel designer chemicals (of which the phenethylamines such as ECSTASY are the best known) but also thousands of organic sources. Some of these are (at least to Western culture), new materials (such as the brain blisteringly potent salvia divinorum, or the gently fuzzy blue lotus of the Nile). Whatever their source, people in the early 21st century, especially in the industrialised world, have access to staggering variety of consciousness altering substances.

We have all those modern alchemists to thank for this situation. Albert Hofmann, father of LSD, and Alexander Shulgin, the godfather of rave culture, who in 1976 synthetized and thoughtfully tested ECSTASY on himself. Many of these discoveries come wrapped in their own synchronistic, some might say magickal, packaging. Hofmann discovered the reality shattering effects of LSD as a result of accidentally ingesting the chemical he was working on. A chemical that he'd created five years before in 1938 (just as World War II was about to kick off).

As the war drew to a close, Hofmann writing in *LSD My Problem Child* says:

"A peculiar presentiment—the feeling that this substance could possess properties other than those established in the first investigations—induced me, five years after the first synthesis, to produce LSD-25 once again so that a sample could be given to the pharmacological department for further tests. This was quite unusual;

experimental substances, as a rule, were definitely stricken from the research program if once found to be lacking in pharmacological interest."

One famous bicycle ride through wonderland later, and the rest as they say, is history. But ah! All those fantastically twisted plot devices! The CIA get interested in LSD as a mind control drug (they'd already been sniffing around, trying to score magick mushrooms with Gordon Wasson's explorations of Mexican shamanism) and so they are the ones that the Gods choose to distribute it to the youth of America. The CIA dump the stuff into the brains of undergraduate research subjects, including people who become counter-cultural icons, such as Ken Kesey. They may also have covertly been bankrolling a Harvard lecturer in psychology, one Timothy Leary. The stable door of modern psychoactive culture was flung open by those very organisations that are now charged with re-capturing the horses that have long since bolted.

So how does this peculiar situation link with contemporary esoteric practice? Much of my own activity, and that of the magicians I've been fortunate to work with, has been about creating new rituals that serve to contain and indeed amplify the new psychoactives that are available today.

Let me give you three examples.

Ketamine – this is a dissociative anaesthetic. It is typically used in anaesthesia of children, the elderly, burns victims and, famously, horses. It's a chemical worth getting to know because it's increasingly used in palliative care. At the end of your life it's quite likely that it will be ketamine that will send you off into the realm of the ancestors. The basic ketamine trip is that of becoming aware of consciousness as it re-emerges. A high enough dose of the drug will knock you out and the trip arises as awareness and memory comes back on line.

Ketamine makes you lose contact with your body. You lose the sense of where you end and, for instance, the curtains begin. So one way we've discovered you can work with this material is through the process of mummification. The participant is naked, then wrapped neck to foot in Clingfilm (black Clingfilm is best). Then a large dose of ketamine is administered by insufflation and the head is then bound with only the nostrils remaining uncovered.

Floating in a memory-less state the participants finds themselves in a world deep underground, rooted in the muladhara chakra's chthonic darkness. The other ritualists judge the time after the ketamine has been taken (perhaps taking low doses themselves) and begin to chant, moving up through the seed syllable mantras of each centre. As memory comes back on line the mummified magician feels their consciousness awakening, dividing from the unified null state. As this happens and the chanting around them builds towards the Sahasrâra so bandage scissors are used to open the cocoon. As the plastic binding falls away so the subject emerges, first imagining themselves as a flowing liquid. Then realising they have limbs, a form, and that they can move in emerging space of separate existences. This ceremony is a powerful initiation; a death and resurrection.

Another type of ritual; this time involving the formidable power of 'toad venom', 5-MeO-DMT which has been (perhaps correctly) described as the most powerful entheogens on the planet. In this ritual the sacrament is central to a rite of trance where the aim is to connect to the life force of the planet. In this ceremony a space is made, ideally outdoors, participants circumambulate the location, each coming forward to partake of the four elements; scented herbs of air, honey for fire, water and the smell of rich earth. Then, on blankets, animal skins and the grass they kneel and the white perfumed smoke of the toad venom is administered. A simple drumbeat and a lilting chant help the psychonauts to dive into the heart of the power in the earth. Rivers of dark DNA swim in front of eyes but there is typically none of the bright visions that the venom's sister chemical (N,N-DMT of Terence McKenna fame) can produce. Instead there is a sense that one is expanding down and simultaneously, outward. Into the cellular heart of creation, out into the radiant void of space and then all around there is nothing but, as Maya Deren brilliantly put it 'the white darkness'.

A final example of an engagement, this time with the aphrodisiac of psychedelic Pan, namely 5-MeO-DiPT or 'foxy methoxy'. A pharmacological sister to DMT, Foxy is so called because of an article in *Playboy Magazine* that favourably commented on its erotic potential. Ideal for tantric sex (as in real tantric sex, you know, with a real partner) this material keeps the body sense intact but allows vibrations of energy to deliciously suffuse the organism. It comes on like Ecstasy, takes you up fast and then dumps you off somewhere that looks a bit like a mushroom trip. Since at low dose the visual disturbance is minimal and cognition remains good this is an ideal sacrament to combine with group ritual, even fairly elaborate processes. I remember a rite to Abraxas featuring an elemental healing process, an invocation of the chicken headed deity and the cracking of a giant golden egg, but that, as they say, is another story…

Now interestingly there are some ways of getting ecstatic which are less fraught with legal problems in our culture. A few years ago I was hanging with two chest piercings through my skin from an ancient yew somewhere on the south coast of England. And it wasn't just me, there were seven of us similarly wounded and dancing, stretching cords from our bodies to a ring of rope round the tree. Leaning backwards, letting the tug of the needles pull at our flesh. For some participants there was plenty of blood.

Funny that if a police officer had walked past it would have been more legitimate to be doing this (although I recognised there is legislation that could have been involved to prosecute us for our English style sundance) than being mummified on ketamine. And why is this? The fact is that we, the industrialised world (and most of the rest of the planet who follow what our governments do) have a deeply abiding fear of drugs.

Now it's true that drugs and drug use are problematic. But making these things illegal, as with alcohol prohibition in the early 20th century in the United States, does not make the problems associated with them go away. In fact it makes things much, much worse. Drugs can be useful in shocking us out of habitual patterns of behaviour, allowing us perceive the world anew. However they can also be cages of drunken violence, of habitation, addiction and sorrow. But it's no news to say that the flip side of heaven is hell or the shadow of ecstasy is despair. The fact is that, as a culture, we need to own this truth, and not keep brushing the white powder under the carpet in the hope that it will go away.

So every time a locus of ecstasy appears in our culture it's stamped on. Not in a big conspiracy way but simply out of habit. Mushrooms go on sale openly in London's Camden market, within months legislation is rushed through to stop it. New chemicals are created with ecstatic and therapeutic potential; they are banned in the blink of an eye. And those most public manifestations of ecstatic society, such as Rave Culture and even latterly pub culture have been outlawed, squeezed and redefined by the state. Personal ecstasy may be dangerous but collective, communal ecstasy is social dynamite!

Why are we, as a society as a species so afraid of this material ecstasy? Is it born from the lingering horror that, in true Tantric style, it is the physical world, in this case chemicals, which are our means of our liberation? We've been told how we need to pray, to do good works, to trust in the Lord, when in fact we can get a reliable religious experience from a good dose of psilocybin and a little appropriate ritualisation? Timothy Leary's research student Walter N. Pahnke, proved this in 1962 when he gave a bunch of divinity students mushrooms in Boston University's chapel, just prior to the Good Friday service. Unsurprisingly (to anyone who has taken this entheogen) all those who were dosed reported profound religious experiences, experiences indistinguishable in their phenomenology from the mystical experiences reported in other contexts. Just to check the results of this experiment (and rather as though the last forty-four years hadn't happened) the experiment was repeated in 2006, and produced exactly the same results.

Communist and capitalist, left and right politicians want to keep prohibition in place. Terence McKenna commented on this, suggesting that it was the radical ontologically unpicking of reality that psychedelic drugs produce that meant the State had to ban them. In common with many other commentators he also pointed out how those drugs that speed the wheels of industry (or the 'means of production' if you prefer) such as caffeine, that take our minds of the dullness of the day (tobacco), or blot out the pointlessness of struggle (booze) are all perfectly acceptable. The general profile, of which psychoactives remain legal, remains unchanged, though the chemicals drafted in service may vary. Of course to calm the masses with opium (like we did in Victorian times) would be terrible; instead we provide Prozac snuggles for downtime and a Red Bull pick-me-up for when the going gets tough.

Frequently voices are raised about this insanity. Most recently a chief science advisor to the British Government lost his position after having the temerity to suggest that taking drugs such as ECSTASY really didn't deserve to be considered as dangerous as some perfectly legal activities. Professor David Nutt, the man in question, described the Kafkaesque process of drug classification in his lecture of July published by the Centre for Crime and Justice Studies at Kings College London:

Member of Parliament "You can't compare harms from a legal activity with an illegal one."

Professor Nutt "Why not?"

Member of Parliament "Because one's illegal."

Professor Nutt "Why is it illegal?"

Member of Parliament "Because it's harmful."

Professor Nutt "Don't we need to compare harms to determine if it should be illegal?"

Member of Parliament "You can't compare harms from a legal activity with an illegal one."

Good grief! No wonder this academic lost his job! He's clearly insane, whereas our wise politician has got a perfect grip on things...

Yet in the British Isles, and round the globe, there are many religions that make use of the ecstatic power of drugs. From the Rastafari movement, orthodox Hinduism, the Peyote users of North and the ayahuasca users of South America. These and many other movements exist which are being informed by the core principles of what Aleister Crowley called Thelema, namely that personal revelation through ecstatic experience is what religion is all about. Not adherence to some garbled Holy Book whether it is *The Koran*, King James or indeed *The Book of the Law*.

So what are we, what are you as magicians doing about this? Make no mistake our time has come. That's why although some of the ecstatic cults are informed by the works of Crowley and Western esoteric culture, many are not. Thelema is one formulation of this psycho-historic force, a force that is popping up in rave culture as much as it is in the burgeoning numbers of the various psychedelic religions. And the tide is turning. The Santo Damie Church and the União do Vegetal, both international religions that use an ayahuasca style brew, have had significant legal victories in the United States and elsewhere. They have won the right to import their DMT rich sacrament into that most prohibitionist of jurisdictions. The changes are coming and they are going to leave groups like the Ordo Templi Orientis and squeaky-clean Wicca behind as quaint anachronisms of muddled Masonry unless they focus their attention on what really matters. What matters is the core spirit of those traditions, the spirit of ecstasy as a valid spiritual path. What matters is changing the law of the land, of maturing as a culture so we can make use of the plethora of psychoactives that we have access to without running screaming into the arms of the Nanny State or addicted oblivion.

This doesn't mean we all have to take drugs. Or indeed that chemical ecstasy is the only true path to enlightenment. But what it does mean is that devotees of this path need to fight for legal acceptance of their activities as a valid spiritual praxis. More broadly our cultures need to embrace the ecstatic as an acceptable and indeed essential human state. A state that should be valued respected and enjoyed.

It can be done. A mere seventy-two years after Oscar Wilde was imprisoned for 'gross indecency' homosexuality was legalised in Britain. This change in the law overturned hundreds of years of criminal and thousands of years of Abrahamic religious law. Such a shocking volte-face is coming and entheogen users should be among those pushing for their own Stonewall riots. The cults of ecstasy are what this aeon is all about, so wise up, get loaded and ditch those holy books! They may have been the spiritual booster rockets that fired us out of earth orbit, but now we need to jettison them. Now the real work begins; it's time to storm the citadel of sobriety and party!

New Age Zombie Apocalypse

The zombie is one of the most pervasive images in modern culture at the dawn of the second decade of the 21st century. They are, quite literally everywhere. Shambling down the street, slack jawed and drooling. Their cry of 'BRAINS! BRAINS!' echoes from the walls of the urban space. Sometimes as part of a protest, sometimes a part of a surrealistic flash mob. Typically the virus (zombism is closely associated with contagion) is most virulent in the young. Spreading like a necrotising infection through teenagers and, remarkably, able to spread via electronic systems. Facebook seems to be a major vector for the infection, watch those status updates change to the moaned cry 'BRAINS! BRAINS!' See as the profile pictures of smiling teens as they are replaced with livid green skinned, sunken-eyed horrors of defiled humanity.

Then there is the blood. Whether smeared on a lab-coat or spotting a wedding dress, zombies leak fluid. This is part of the clear evidence not only of living death but also of the decay, which they exemplify. Whereas the rest of us usually try to keep our body fluids locked away the zombie will, without any shame (hey, they're dead after all!), gush and drip and besmirch everything in their vicinity. Spittle and nasal mucus are often in evidence, but it's the blood that gets star billing.

University departments and even local authorities draw up slightly tongue-in-cheek plans for what to do in the event of zombie attack. Certain times of the year see more outbreaks than others. Summer in Britain brings various zombie parades and gatherings to many urban areas. But of course the infection is at its worst as the weather changes, autumn comes, and the season of Halloween begins.

Zombies over the Rainbow

One of the most fascinating stories about zombies is told by the Canadian anthropologist, ethnobotanist, author and photographer Wade Davis. Author of a number of excellent books his 1985 bestseller *The Serpent and the Rainbow* recounts his explorations of the Haitian zombie phenomena. Davis suggests that zombies are created in part by the use of tetrodotoxin, the pharmacologically active agent found in the body of the puffer fish. Tetrodotoxin or TTX can produce sialorrhea (excessive production of saliva), sweating, headache, weakness, lethargy, incoordination, tremor, paralysis, cyanosis (skin turning blue), aphonia (inability to speak), seizures, dyspnoea (shortness of breath), coughing, and dizziness. A dramatic drop in respiratory rate may occur, in some cases leading to coma and death. There is no known antidote.

Although tetrodotoxin is found in several aquatic animals is most famously present in puffer fish used to produce fugu, the potentially deadly Japanese delicacy. The toxin is actually produced by a symbiotic bacteria, which lives in these animals. Of course when fugu is prepared the skill of the chef is to remove those areas in which the level of TTX is dangerous but not to remove it all. It is the buzz, which very low levels of TTX induce, that makes this dangerous cuisine so appealing. In fact it's debatable whether one should consider fugu as an exotic fried fish supper or a powerful psychoactive drug.

Another potentially terrifying effect of TTX is that it does not cross the blood–brain barrier, leaving the victim fully conscious while paralysing the muscles. According to Wade Davis it is this effect that is used to make people appear to be dead. After being buried, immobilised but still fully conscious, the victim is dug up from their grave by the Haitian sorcerer. The psychological trauma of the event, perpetuated by putting the hapless victim on a madness-maintaining regular dose of datura, continues this living death. Occasionally zombies turn up again in villages, sometimes months or even years after they have been buried. Some people of course escape their pharmacological prison, but those who are glimpsed while still in the full thrall of their new master would certainly appear 'undead'.

Why the outbreak of zombies now in the second decade of the 21st century? Perhaps it is an acting out of our fear of epidemics, of diseases which these days can get on-board aircraft and be half way round the world before you can say 'historically-overdue-mass-influenza epidemic'. Then there is the fear of the brainless mass of humanity. All those people you see but don't know who crowd onto trains and buses and, it would seem, mindlessly pilot their automobiles around the city, day in, day out. Are they really sentient humans or Matrix-like illusions?

Derridan zombies, like people, only not *really* people. As the population on earth breaches 7,000,000,000 these shambling hunks of meat seem to swarm everywhere.

Our cultural estrangement from the physical fact of death could be some of it. Most of us hardly get to see dead bodies these days, even the animal bodies for our food come surgically sliced and transmogrified into 'nuggets' and 'mince'. Dead loved ones are spirited away in the night in thick impenetrable body bags and the next time we 'see' them it's usually shut inside a box. As the celebrant pushes the big green button the opaque casket glides out of the room and those little curtains shut. No sign of bodies burning, no sound from the whirring cremulator, no metallic clanking as the metal of replacement hips is recovered from the still warm ash.

Rather than desiccated, disinfected ashes the zombies remind us of the visceral nature of death. All that discharge and goo, the moaning and the pain, not just of death itself but also of the gradual debilitation that we imagine from ageing and illness. Zombies are sickness writ large. Finally we could consider the fact that those people who are now in the teens and twenties are children of a generation many of whom may have encountered rave, and more generally modern drug culture. Perhaps in the minds of those zombified kids are half-remembered images of Mum battered out of her head on pills, arriving back from the club while they were sitting with the babysitter watching TV? Or could it have been that time you saw Dad, when he was the worse for a night on the tiles and a morning on the special K?

Zombie Flashmob Attack

It was bonfire night and we're meeting in a fabulous esoteric art gallery not far from the white and red springs in Glastonbury. Given our location it was inevitable that we'd have to perform a ritual that required climbing the Tor and so the Zombie Apocalypse was created. Once again the technique being used was that of embodying that which one wishes to change, and undergoing a ritualised transformation towards what one hopes to achieve. The methodology was intended to work at both a personal and collective level. Devised by Soror Res and myself this would be a ritual to encourage critical thinking within the New Age movement. And, speaking as magicians meeting in Glastonbury, this enchantment of critical thinking should apply equally to us as to what I might consider the laughable mystical woo-woo pedalled by some of the magick shops on Glastonbury's High Street.

So the rubric for the ceremony was simple. We'd dress up as zombies and walk into the heart of the New Age, Glastonbury Tor which, as I'm sure you know, is considered by many people to be the heart chakra of Gaia. Searching in our crippled zombie fashion for 'BRAINS!', we would ascend the Tor and, at the top, destroy a copy of an influential contemporary New Age book. Once this was completed we magically find our brains and would return, down the Tor, having erudite and intellectually rigorous conversations. We'd transform the mindless New Age zombie into an actively intelligent human.

The text that we planned to destroy was one that Soror Res had, manfully, read from cover to cover. It was one of those books that ranged across shamanism, psychedelic experience, UFO abductions and the like and, while it had many good points, had fallen in her view at the final hurdle. Rather than see the phenomena it documented as being perhaps many manifestations arising from a shared human physiology of altered states of consciousness, the author had been marshalling their evidence to provide the evidential glue to stick together an otherwise insubstantial theory. This theory was that millennia ago aliens had arrived on earth and engineered our DNA, leaving a method for getting in touch with them, outside space and time, encoded in our biology.

Now there are several problems with this theory. I'm sure that you, gentle reader, are quite aware of many of them without the need for me to disentangle the story, or cut things up with Occam's razor on your behalf. But beyond the view that the theory simply doesn't hold together is a broader point about the New Age movement. We must be able to entertain ideas in our lives to ask 'what if...?' and to play with possibilities, even ones that may seem far-fetched. The history of human innovation demonstrates that, if we become blinkered into one way of thinking, we may miss out on many wonderful things. But, as they say, if you open your mind too much your brain will fall out. We need our critical abilities, our ability to dissect arguments and when we present theories we need to honestly engage with ideas like proof, truth, evidence and falsifiability.

If, for instance, you want to 'literally' suggest that physical aliens came to earth thousands of years ago to hide their brand name in the genetic sequence of early humans, you better have some pretty good positive evidence (rather than circumstantial stuff which is open to a range of much more probable explanations). There is nothing wrong with this reading of events as metaphor. Certainly one might convincingly argue (as Terence McKenna does in *Food of the Gods*) that psychedelic experience accelerated the development of culture in the human species. But literal space ships coming through space, while logically possible, is more likely to be the result of a series of a priori assumptions than a sound assessment of the data. Erich von Daniken's suggestion that the Nazca lines were landing markers for alien visitors, because of their apparent similarity to modern landing strips for aircraft, comes to mind. Apart from anything else when did you last see a flying saucer than needed a runway?

This kind of literalism, in my view, demonstrates a lack of intellectual subtlety and a failure to see beyond the surface of things. Sure when you take a hit of DMT you might meet aliens who seem utterly real and tell you they have been doing a mash-up edit of your DNA code since way before Lascaux. However just because something as impressive as a DMT elf tells you this doesn't make it true. By all means explore the idea but please leave it open to question, reinterpretation and indeed abandonment. I'm reminded an account by Michael Harner of what happened after one his first ayahuasca visions:

"I was now eager to solicit a professional opinion from the most supernaturally knowledgeable of the Indians, a blind shaman who had made many excursions into the spirit world with the aid of the ayahuasca drink. It seemed only proper that a blind man might be able to be my guide to the world of darkness. I went to his hut, taking my notebook with me, and described my visions to him segment by segment. At first I told him only the highlights; thus, when I came to the dragon-like creatures, I skipped their arrival from space and only said, "There were these giant black animals, something like great bats, longer than the length of this house, who said that they were the true masters of the world." There is no word for dragon in Conibo, so 'giant bat' was the closest I could come to describe what I had seen.

He stared up toward me with his sightless eyes, and said with a grin, "Oh, they're always saying that. But they are only the Masters of Outer Darkness."

The moral of this story is that, of course, the spirits can and do lie!

The Hills are Undead with the sound of Zombies

Shambling through the bonfire night air there is a motley crocodile of zombies. Careering into lampposts, drooling, moaning again and again 'BRAINS!' We are led by a Brother who is wearing a high viability jacket of fluorescent yellow and bearing in large letters the word 'Wizard'. He leads the procession and, with video camera in hand, is our guide, alibi (we're doing a film for YouTube), and ritual recorder or scribe. He also clutches a copy of the book, which is destined for destruction, and this is the strange zombie-attractor that leads us up the hill.

We ascend, some faster than others. There is much falling over and dragging of limbs. The sacramental nature of the ritual also makes the climb a formidable challenge for some of our party.

After the steep initial ascent we arrive at the gradually inclining path, sloping gently up towards St. Michael's tower which crowns the summit of the Tor. There are sheep grazing on the grass slopes but our cries of 'BRAINS!' are only mildly disturbing to them. After all these are Glastonbury sheep and have probably seen a fair number of odd goings on in their time.

Arriving at the top zombies begin to bounce off the walls, getting stuck and flailing like failing automata in the doorways to the tower. As more of us arrive the flickering torches reveal a space full of what appear to be horribly injured, profoundly disabled people. Limbs twitch, mouths gape and eyes roll empty and vacant upwards.

The book is produced and crying 'BRAINS! BRAINS! BRAINS!' We fall upon it, ripping it and screwing up the pages. (These fragments are scrupulously collected for responsible disposal after the ritual.)

Soror Res picks up a ripped page and begins to read. It's an observation on the analysis of the ayahuasca experience by a noted researcher in the field. She reads it and begins to contradict what it says. I chime in the fact that I've met the researcher in question and that the book is clearly misrepresenting his views. All around drooling idiots have been replaced by brains that are razor sharp engines of analysis and questioning.

Fireworks are lit and the Tor bursts into multi-coloured light. Our cohort are standing normally again, chatting and talking to the small number of locals that are sat on the slopes of the Tor that evening. The mindless zombies are banished.

Epilogue

It was about three months later I chanced on a Youtube video showing the author of the volume we'd destroyed in conversation with some *aficionados* from the current psychedelic scene. From what he said it seem to suggest that our ritual had been a success since he'd developed a more critical (or perhaps open) position on the meaning of the DMT experience. I'd also been attacking my own a priori assumption that magick works by reading *The Believing Brain: From Ghosts and Gods to Politics and Conspiracies - How We Construct Beliefs and Reinforce Them as Truths* by Michael Shermer. As a result I've made a few significant re-considerations of my thoughts about the meaning, social role and effectiveness of magick. Which, in a paradoxical way, demonstrates to me that magick does indeed, sometimes, work.

Chaos Buddha Rite

This ritual was developed by Frater Pelagius.

Purpose
A Working to help us uncover an understanding of Self that allows us to dance with the playfulness and uncertainty of life!

A. An invocation to the Chaos Buddha

B. The three vows

C. The offering of practice-20 minutes of guided sitting and then x8 intoned 'Chaos Buddha'

Invocation:
We call to you O great bellied Chaos Buddha....

The laughing Buddha- representing the Erisian/Discordian stream of the Chaos impulse. A trickster Buddha who invites us to relax into our conflicts, to breath into them, to half-smile, to release them to the deeper aspects of ourselves- to subvert our linear, rational attempts to make things work. Chaos emanates from a belly that bespeaks enjoyment, pleasure and playfulness-rather than asceticism, sacrifice and denial. A place of succulence, opulence and contentment. An earthy bass note that challenges the belief that Wisdom is a move away from matter. A playful monkey Buddha pinching Tripitaka's bottom. A Zen rebel, taking us ever back to the circle rather than the straight line.

Hail the Chaos Buddha!

The Three Chaos Buddha Treasures:
I bow to the Chaos Buddha as the half-smiling fool!"

I bow to the Dharmic paradox that there may be no absolute truth!

I bow to the tribe of Holy Idiots bold enough to do the Work of Magick!

The Offering of Practice

20 minutes of led mindfulness practice - giving explanation of observing the breath, noticing and describing thoughts, feelings and sensations. The aim of this process is NOT to change anything. It is not to strive for one-pointed awareness or any trance state. Mindfulness or insight meditation is about observing one's usual state of awareness, noticing how we become absorbed in our internal dialogue and can return again to an anchor in the present (generally the breath). The dance between these states is the practise. A wandering mind is not a failure. We smile to ourselves that wise knowing smile of the Enlightened One, amused to notice that this wandering is simply the nature of the mind. We are compassionate with ourselves, not striving after 'success', and return our awareness gently to the breath in the present moment.

During the meditation a few reminders are given ("return to the breath, easily in this moment" etc) to assist in the recollection of 'now' and a reminder to awaken from the internal dialogue in which we may have become engrossed.

The singing bowl is sounded to mark the end of the meditative practice.

All stand and face the image of the Chaos Buddha.

Intone the words 'Chaos Buddha' seven times, then, holding hands an eighth time. Find a Chaos Buddha on the other side of the circle and go and give them some love!

Banish with laughter (and more hugging)!

Fig 12 The Chaos Buddha.

Intensify the Normal

As magicians we should aim for at least one ecstatic moment each day. This of course doesn't mean that a day without some full-on practice is day wasted. For Austin Spare, those occultists who limit their magick to symbolic acts within ceremony are missing out. "Their practices prove their incapacity; they have no magick to intensify the normal, the joy of a child or healthy person, none to evoke their pleasure or wisdom from themselves."

So today I was walking across the 13th century bridge that spans the river where I live. It was early morning and the rose-pink sky was being echoed in the silvery water of the river at high tide. The water seemed thicker, an effect that seemed to be caused by the low temperature. Like quicksilver the river ran slow, spinning in vortices as it passed beneath the arches of the bridge. Birds were starting their day and slipping silent through the clear air. Smoke crawled from a few chimneys and early morning cars prowled the streets.

I am located in this landscape. I know its history and its people. I have my own memories, joyful and painful, located in this place. My breath is easy and I find myself stopping for a moment by the quay and looking out towards the old shipyard and beyond to where my river curves round to meet her sister (the river Taw) as together they unite with the sea.

I am, for a moment, transported into that hyper-reality which always, on reflection, makes me think I've stepped into a frame from a graphic novel. There is a razor sharpness to my senses and I am both observer and at one with the world I inhabit. I feel profoundly grateful that I am able to experience this moment.

Just before I go into the gallery where I'm working I notice how the grass beneath my feet bends. I've deliberately walked off the path in order to enjoy this sensation.

Yes all our ceremonial work, our yoga and study matters - but only if it increases our capacity to enjoy the normal that bit more.

Sources

The Pain of Division, was initial offering for the Scarlet Imprint collection *XVI*. The Sabbat of Chaos, was an essay requested by *Pagan Dawn magazine* as an introduction to the chaos style of magick. Mastering Witchcraft was a course delivered at arcanoriumcollege.com. Dredd Lord of the Shadows, became part of *The Book of Baphomet*. The Discovery of Witchcraft: appeared in the academic collection *The New Generation Witches: Teenage Witchcraft in Contemporary Culture (Controversial New Religions)* by Hannah E. Johnston and Peg Aloi. Watching the apocalypse, was contributed to the collection *The Enduring Problems with Prophecy: from Early-Modern Times to 2012 and Beyond*, edited by Dave Evans. The Rite to Roam, appeared in *The Wanton Green*, edited by Gordon MacLellan. Baphomet Rising, was published in *SilkMilk* Spool#4 edited by Orryelle Defenestrate-Bascule. The Pope & The Prophet, was published at theblogofbaphomet.com. Beyond the Pharmakon, was a lecture in the series hosted by David Luke entitled *Ecology, Cosmos and Consciousness* at The October Gallery, London. Return to Chaos, appeared in *Pentacle Magazine* in advance of The Colours of Chaos event in London, 2008. The Black Flag & The Mystery: Anarchy in the Everyday. is inspired by *325 magazine*. Lessons from the Witches, was created for the 60th Anniversary publication *The Museum of Witchcraft A Magical History*. Wine & Strange Drugs. is based on my lecture at the 13th International Thelemic Symposium in Oxford, 2009, this essay was the one that finally appeared in the Scarlet Imprint volume *XVI*. New Age Zombie Apocalypse & Intensify the Normal, first appeared on theblogofbaphomet.com

Notes & Bibliography

To Chapter Discovering Witchcraft:

1 Double quote marks indicate direct quotes from Dawn. This research was conducted by audio taped interview at Dawn's home in North Devon, UK. The sections in this essay reflect approximate order in which our conversation developed. This interview is closer to a spontaneous dialogue between two equal practitioners of the Craft rather than a structured ethnographic interview.

2 Eg: Sorita and Dave Rankine see http://www.avalonia.co.uk/contact/sorita_david.htm

3 Satanic ritual abuse (SRA), refers to the belief that an organized network of Satanists engages in brainwashing and abusing victims, especially children. Claims of Satanic Ritual Abuse remain controversial and law enforcement sources, criminologists, psychologists, and religious affairs commentators generally consider this belief false. The moral panic created by the SRA scare developed in the early 1980s in the USA and arrived in the UK after American ritual abuse 'experts' helped spread the hoax to the United Kingdom. Seminars given to police groups and social service agencies triggered many Multi-Victim, Multi-Offender (MVMO) cases (e.g. Bishop Auckland, Cleveland, Newcastle, Nottingham, Rochdale, Orkney and Pembroke). Some of these British MVMO cases resulted in dismissal of all charges or acquittals. But others sent pr. The Health Secretary of the British government, Mrs. Virginia Bottomley, ordered a study of ritual abuse in 1991, after a number of children were taken into care in Rochdale and Orkney during a panic by social workers. Professor Jean La Fontaine headed a team at Manchester University, which evaluated all known British ritual abuse cases. She issued her report in 1994. The conclusion of the report was that no evidence exists for Satanic Ritual Abuse in England.

4 Big Brother is a UK television game show in which contestants live together in a shared house under constant surveillance by TV camera. Contestants rely, in part, on public votes to stay in the house and thereby win a cash prize.

5 Ironically a magick spell to curse someone represents a greater source of power in a culture such a contemporary Western culture which (legally) does not believe in the power of curses. In such an environment causing death by magick is effectively the perfect crime. However in other cultures other esoteric specialists would exist to identify the person originating the curse and to act to stop them, often with 'extreme prejudice'.

6 For those who may have missed this one, the relevant episode is Bewitched, Bothered And Bewildered - Episode 28, First aired February 10, 1998. Xander tries to use Valentine's Day to further his relationship with Cordelia but she succumbs to peer pressure and breaks up with him. With the help of Amy (who is exploring her mother's witch powers), he puts a love spell on her which goes horribly wrong, turning him into every woman's desire; except Cordelia's.

7 See http://www.witchfest.net/

8 A UK based Pagan networking and support organisation established in 1971. Citations

Bibliography
Printed material

Beth, Rae, *Hedge Witch*, Robert Hale 1992
Buckland, Raymond, *The Tree Red* Wheel/Weiser, 1984
Crowley, Aleister, *777*, Red Wheel/Weiser 1987
Crowley, Vivienne, *Wicca: The Old Religion in the New Age* Aquarian Press, 1989
Cunningham, Scot, *Incenses, Oils and Brews* and Llewellyn 1989
Cunningham, Scot *Crystal, Gem and Metal Magick* Llewellyn   1988

Cunningham, Scot *Earth, Air, Fire and Water - More Techniques of Natural Magick* Llewellyn 1992

Davies, Owen *Cunning-folk: Popular Magick in English History* Hambledon & London Ltd 2003

Gaiman, Neil *The Sandman* (comic) Vertigo launched 1989

Green, Marion *A Witch Alone* . HarperCollins, 2002

Holland, Eileen, *The Wicca Handbook* Red Wheel/Weiser 2000

Lafontaine, J.S., *Extent & Nature of Organized Ritual Abuse* [Great Britain] Department of Health 1994

Leek, Sybil *Diary of a Witch*. Signet Books 1968

Leek, Sybil, *The Complete Art of Witchcraft*, Signet Books 1991

Mathers, S.L. *The Greater Key of Solomon*, R A Kessinger Publishing Co 1997

Mathers, S.L. *The Book of the Sacred Magick of Abra-Melin the Mage* Dover Publications 1975

Murray, Margaret *God of the Witches* Pocket Press 2001

Murray, Margaret, *Witch Cult in Western Europe: A Study in Anthropology* R A Kessinger Publishing Co 1921

Symonds, *John The Great Beast*, Roy Publishers, 1952

Valiente, Doreen *Witchcraft for Tomorrow,* Hale 1978

Lens based material

Buffy the Vampire Slayer UPN First aired March 1997

Charmed Spelling Television First aired October 1998

The Craft, Directed by Andrew Fleming 1996

The Crow Directed by Alex Proyas 1994

The Moon Stallion Written by Brian Hayle for BBC Television 1978

Mandrake

'Books you don't see everyday'

Bright From the Well by Dave Lee
978-1869928-841, £10.99

'Bright From the Well' consists of five stories plus five essays and a rune-poem. The stories revolve around themes from Norse myth - the marriage of Frey and Gerd, the story of how Gullveig-Heidh reveals her powers to the gods, a modern take on the social-origins myth Rig's Tale, Loki attending a pagan pub moot and the Ragnarok seen through the eyes of an ancient shaman.

The essays include examination of the Norse creation or origins story, of the magician in or against the world and a chaoist's magical experiences looked at from the standpoint of Northern magic.'

'Dave Lee coaches breathwork, writes fiction and non-fiction, blends incenses and oils, creates music and collages'

The Apophenion: A Chaos Magic Paradigm by Peter J Carroll
978-1869928-421, £10.99

My final Magnum Opus if its ideas remain unfalsified within my lifetime, otherwise its back to the drawing board. Yet I've tried to keep it as short and simple as possible, it consists of eight fairly brief and terse chapters and five appendices.

It attacks most of the great questions of being, free will, consciousness, meaning, the nature of mind, and humanity's place in the cosmos, from a magical perspective. Some of the conclusions seem to challenge many of the deeply held assumptions that our culture has taught us, so brace yourself for the paradigm crash and look for the jewels revealed in the wreckage.

This book contains something to offend everyone; enough science to upset the magicians, enough magic to upset the scientists, and enough blasphemy to upset most trancendentalists.

"The most original, and probably the most important, writer on Magick since Aleister Crowley."

-Robert Anton Wilson, author of the *Cosmic Trigger* trilogy.

Other Mandrake Titles:
Fries/*Cauldron of the Gods: a manual of Celtic Magick.*
552pp, royal octavo, 9781869928612 £24.99$40 paper

Fries/*Seidways Shaking, Swaying and Serpent Mysteries.* 350pp 9781869928360 £15/$25
Still the definitive and much sought after study of magical trance and possession techniques.

Fries/*Helrunar - a manual of rune magick.* 454pp 9781968828902 pbk, £19.99/$40 Over 130 illustrations. new enlarged and improved edition
'...eminently practical and certainly breaks new ground.' - Ronald Hutton

Fries/*Visual Magick: a manual of freestyle shamanism.* 196pp 9781869928575 £10.99/$20. *'A practical modern grimoire.'* The Cauldron

Wilson *I, Crowley - Last Confession of the Beast 666 - Almost* £9.99/$20 250 pages ISBN 9781869928544, second edition
'Brilliant . . . the Great Beast explaining himself in lapel-grabbing prose.' Simon Callow

Order direct from

Mandrake of Oxford
PO Box 250, Oxford, OX1 1AP (UK)
Phone: 01865 243671
(for credit card sales)
Prices include economy postage
Visit our web site
online at - www.mandrake.uk.net

www.ingramcontent.com/pod-product-compliance
Lightning Source LLC
Chambersburg PA
CBHW071426160426
43195CB00013B/1820